"Sometimes I feel like a blob"—
This was one comment that turned
up on a confidential questionnaire.
A teen-ager wrote it—and he went
on to say "I don't know who or
what I am or what I'm here for. I
can't seem to get identified."
The greatest problem of a young
person is to find the answers to
these questions.

In this book, the author discusses
these questions, and wisely deals
with many of the problems commonly
faced by young people today. And
though she does not claim to have
all the answers, she insists (in a
highly practical and extremely
palatable way) that God does.

ETHEL BARRETT

Sometimes I Feel Like a BLOB

G/L REGAL BOOKS

A Division of G/L Publications
Glendale, California, U.S.A.

Over 170,000 in print

Second Printing, 1966
Third Printing, 1966
Fourth Printing, 1967
Fifth Printing, 1968
Sixth Printing, 1968
Seventh Printing, 1969
Eighth Printing, 1970
Ninth Printing, 1972
Tenth Printing, 1973
Eleventh Printing, 1974
Twelfth Printing, 1976

Published by

Regal Books Division, G/L Publications
Glendale, California 91209 U.S.A.
ISBN 0-8307-0015-3

To Marianne McBain Barrett

Contents

"Who

am

I?"

Who are you indeed? Who are you that God should be interested in you? Well, it is something to consider.

From the pen of the great historian Herodotus, comes the strange tale of a king. As strange and interesting as this tale is, it would not concern us except that it pictures the probable boyhood of a man who later appears in the Old Testament, and who is very important in God's plan, because he —

Well.

Any "probable" boyhood of a man who later got to be in the Bible is important. But the point is, before he got to be in the Bible, who **was** he?

Well, he was a prince, according to history. And his uncle wanted him killed. And he ordered him to be taken up to the mountainside to be devoured by wild animals, his necklace to be brought back as proof that he was dead. But his uncle's general took compassion on him at the last moment, and switched him with the dead baby of a goatherd—and brought back the necklace of the prince along with the dead body of the goatherd's baby and, well, you can see that it was all quite complicated. The king was fooled into thinking that Cyrus was dead.

But according to secular history, Cyrus was not dead at all, and later went back to live in his uncle's court under circumstances too complicated to relate here . . . and he later got to make history. For he was the king who "passed the hat" for the Jews to go back and build up their temple.

But the real point of the story is, that after Cyrus got to be in the Bible, it turned out that the Lord had known him all along.

"I, the Lord, which call thee by thy name, am the God of Israel" . . .

He knows you. He can call you by name. Can you put your faith in a greater power?

. . . I, the LORD, which call thee by thy name, am the God of Israel. (Isa. 45:3)

11

"Sometimes I feel like a Blob"

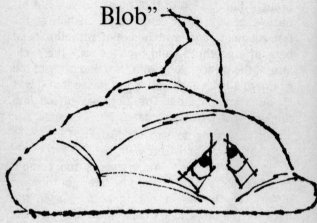

This was one comment that turned up on a confidential questionnaire. A teen-ager wrote it and he went on to say, "I don't know who or what I am or what I'm here for. I can't seem to get identified." The greatest problem of a teen-ager is to find out who he is.

But on with Cyrus. He had no idea that **God** had had a hand in his life. He did not, as yet, even know God. But after he had diverted the Euphrates river, marched into Babylon under the city gates on the dry river bed — the biggest strategic feat in history according to secular historians — and conquered Babylon — what happened?

He found out that God had been there all the time. For what does God say, after Cyrus had cut his swath, made his goal, was the conqueror? "I will go before thee, and make the crooked places straight: I will break in pieces the gates of brass, and cut in sunder the bars of iron: And I will give thee the treasures of darkness, and hidden riches of secret places, that thou mayest know that I, the LORD, which call thee by thy name, am the God of Israel" (Isaiah 45:2,3).

Well.

So God called him by name. And Cyrus thought, up to this point, that he had done it all by himself.

"Who am I?" Who are you? You are the one whom God knows well, even before you were born. He has even called you by name. He knows you through and through . . . And no matter what you do, as you think, on your own, you will find that He was there all the time. Indeed, He was there before you ever did it, whatever it is, for in Isaiah 45:3 He says to Cyrus, " . . . that thou mayest know that I, the LORD, which call thee by thy name, am the God of Israel." And in verse 4, " . . . I have even called mine elect, I have even called thee by thy name: I have surnamed thee, though thou hast not known me . . . "

Who are you? Well, you might not know, but God knows . . . and He will show you. For He knew you before you were born . . . and He has a plan for your life . . . And He will " . . . go before thee and make the crooked places straight."

I will go before thee, and make the crooked places straight: I will break in pieces the gates of brass, and cut in sunder the bars of iron. (Isa. 45:2)

"Supposing I

did decide

to have

a regular

prayer time?"

That seems ridiculous at first. You DO. You ARE. You are reading, well all right, skimming this page right now. And you'll quickly note the Scripture that goes with it, and think about it all the way down to breakfast. And so your daily devotions will have been accomplished.

Now "devotions" is sort of a diluted word. It dilutes what prayer time really is. And makes it a kind of package deal, your little "thought for the day" — all there and very pat. Add to it a verse of Scripture and there you have it — instant spirituality.

It sounds all right — we have instant everything else. And we ARE living at a mad pace these days. What with homework and band practice and clubs and cheer-leading and socials et cetera ad nauseum, there aren't enough hours in the day as it is!

It's true. But the best that can be said for that type of packaged devotions is — it's better than nothing. And God wants more from you than that. But more important — God wants more OF you than that. He wants you to spend more time with Him, concentrating on Him, listening to what He wants to tell you. It takes time. And it will cost something.

There was a preacher once who had this problem. Oh, he prayed regularly all right — but one night he got to thinking about setting aside a regular prayer time and then the question of time came up and right on the heels of that came the question of COST. For with his busy schedule, if he was really going to do the thing right it was going to cost him something.

He got to thinking about it, of all times, while he was watching TV. He was watching the late show and he suddenly got up and turned it off and he watched the picture fade and then he watched the little white spot in the middle and then he stared at the idiot-box after the white spot was gone. And then he thought — "I wonder what would happen if I stopped watching the idiot-box and spent that time with God?"

Well you can see right off that it was going to cost him something. It was going to cost him the late show. But somehow, the minute he made up his mind, he didn't think of it as a "cost" at all — in fact the idea was suddenly so exciting he was

15

amazed that he had waited so long to think of it. It was so stimulating he acted upon it at once — that very night.

The upshot was that his life was changed. In fact God shook his life to its very foundations — and in a way he had not expected. For God led him into the slum districts of New York and opened the way for him to talk to "gangs" of teen-agers who were getting into the most sordid kinds of trouble. And they walked right out of trouble and into the arms of God. It's a long story. He wrote about it in "The Cross and the Switchblade."

But the point is — his life was changed. And the great work he started is still going on, bigger than ever. And all because he decided to give up something else and spend that time having a regular prayer time with God!

God wants more of you. He tells you to "seek the Lord and His strength" (I Chronicles 16:11). He wants to listen to you. He wants to talk to you. And the only way you can have this two-way conversation with Him is through a regular prayer time. And, like the preacher, the minute you make up your mind—you won't think of the cost at all.

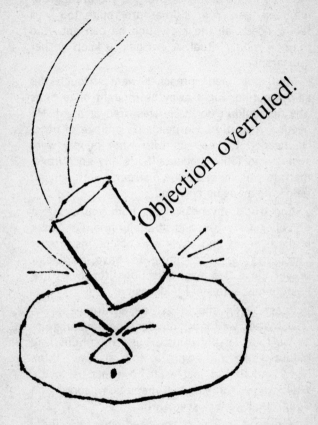

So you've made up your mind to have a regular prayer time? And if you have, the idea suddenly seems exciting. The possibilities are endless. And then, almost at once come the objections. A dozen or more reasons why you cannot squeeze the time out of your busy day. And if you concentrate on it you can think of a million. You need that extra half-hour, well even fifteen minutes' sleep in the morning. And you must get to bed on time at night. After all, you **are** a growing teen-ager. Your studies are rough too — a fellow needs all the recreation he can get. And the hair-rolling ritual. A girl has to keep up her appearance.

Well, this poor preacher went through the same routine. Right away he thought of reasons why he couldn't do it. He was tired at night. He needed relaxation. He needed a change of pace. He needed to keep up with what people were seeing and talking about. If it's any encouragement to you, he had quite a struggle with himself before he made up his mind.

And if it's any help at all, both you and that preacher are at the end of a long line. For Satan is there, ready and eager with objections for any Christian who is deciding to have a regular prayer time. He has objections for everyone, custom-made, to suit the occasion.

"Lest Satan should get an advantage of us ... " When we think of his getting advantage of us we think of big things, big temptations, big failures. Like the slogan in the ads, we "think big." And that is just what he wants us to do. While we're "thinking big" he is busy working on things that, to us, seem little.

You need your rest. You need your recreation. You need to roll up your hair. And so your little list of innocent objections piles up. And if he can get you there, he has got you at the very foundation of your Christian life.

You can't have a friendship with a person you

know just slightly and never take the time to talk to. And you can't have a personal relationship with God if you've just heard about Him but have never taken the trouble to talk with Him or listen to Him.

So, "objection overruled!" Say it. Say it to yourself. Say it aloud. Ask God to help you mean it. And be done with the nonsense that's threatening to keep you from the most wonderful experience of your life.

So you've made up your mind to have a regular prayer time? ALL objections overruled! Now be at it, and God bless you!

Lest Satan should get an advantage of us: for we are not ignorant of his devices. (II Cor. 2:11)

"Why can't I do anything right?"

There's a story about the little boy whose friend got in trouble. When he asked "why?" there was this discussion about the friend's parents, who were not quite what they should be. And the little boy burst out passionately, "If parents are always to blame, how far back does it STOP? Parents had parents too. And the parents' parents had parents. As far back as you can go EVERYBODY had parents. Wow, that's putting all the blame on Adam and Eve!"

Exactly.

When God created the world it was perfect. When He made man and gave him a mate, they were perfect. They had unbroken friendship with God. There was only one thing God told Adam and

Eve they could not do. Exactly what it was is not the point. The point is God said "Don't do it" and Satan said "Do it" and they did it. And in doing it, they took themselves out of God's hands. They were lost. That is what being "lost" is — out of God's hands. And so everyone who was born after that was also out of God's hands.

And in "due time" — that is, the right time, when God was ready, He sent Jesus Christ to die for this "lost" mankind. He was punished in the place of every "lost" person. This was God's gift to every person born. Your privilege as a person is to accept this gift and thereby put yourself back **into** God's hands. That's what being "saved" is. That's what makes you a Christian.

But it doesn't make you perfect.

No person will be perfect until Christ comes again. The old nature you were born with is still there. Blame it on Adam and Eve if you will. But don't be discouraged by it. For when you became a Christian, God gave you a **new** nature. And that is the one you should be concerned about. You are in God's hands, where you belong, where He wants you. And He has promised that your new nature will have victory over the old one. "But thanks be to God which giveth us the victory through our Lord Jesus Christ . . . "

Claim this promise. Confess your failures to God. Then **leave** your failures with God. And then get going. Today is another day!

But thanks be to God, which giveth us the victory through our Lord Jesus Christ. (I Cor. 15:57)

"But I'm not the type"

Go out on deputation work? Door-to-door canvassing? Well, the young people can do that sort of thing if they want to — but leave me out. It's a noble cause I know — but honestly! I'll be happy to help with the socials, take my stint in leading the meetings or, well, I don't want just the fun jobs either — I'll be happy to be on clean-up committees even. But that other stuff — well, it isn't that I'm not willing to work — I'm just completely unsuited for that sort of thing. You know?

Yes.

Perhaps you are. And if you are and that's all there is to it, you have a legitimate gripe. But if you have any deep-down twinges of guilt about it, if you find yourself too much on the defensive about it, and a little too eager and lengthy in excuses — the chances are that God has been speaking to you. If this is the case, the fact that you are "completely unsuited" is, face it, beside the point.

In the book, "The Cross and the Switchblade," there was some deputation work to be done that involved a great deal of canvassing. Some of it was door to door, but most of it was "gang to gang." And the gangs were the most vicious in New York's worst sections. Even the police did not go into their territory except in pairs. But guess whom God chose to go to them alone, unarmed, and at first, unaided? A country preacher who had never been in the big city in his life before. Who did not know his way around. Who did not have any "in." Who was as skinny as the "before" part of the bar-bell ads. Who was, in short, completely "unsuited." He just wasn't the type! **Him** do **that** sort of work for the Lord? Ridiculous.

But he did. Because God called him.

The point is not whether you are the type. The point is — does God want you to do it? If He does — He will **enable** you.

And I thank Christ Jesus our Lord, who hath enabled me, for that he counted me faithful . . .
(I Tim. 1:12)

"I'd
rather
do
it
myself!"

And then there was the television commercial—
"Please — I'd rather do it myself!" It's been
spoofed, imitated, used in jokes and skits — and
for a time it threatened to outdo "Meanwhile,
back at the ranch."

Well, you **want** to "do it yourself." That's the
way you were trained from babyhood. From the

moment you took your first spill — after you'd graduated from babyhood to childhood — and your parents, instead of running to pick you up, told you to do it yourself, you got the idea. It was just the thing to do.

"But," you say, "doesn't God want me to be independent, stand on my own?" Of course He does. He wants you to grow up, stand up, measure up, and all the rest of it. And that's the point. You can't do it, according to His standards, by yourself.

There's a story of a girl who wanted a graduation dress. She went on a shopping spree — and ended in dismay. There was nothing that she could possibly afford. So she decided to make the dress herself. Well, she pinned and basted and matched notch AA to notch ZZ and gathered between the perforations and all the rest of it. And when she finished, it drooped where it should have slooped and fit her like a shower curtain. At the proper moment, when she was ready to die of despair, her fairy godmother appeared. And the proper thing happened, as it always does in fairy tales. They went on another shopping spree — and this time the girl came home with the most beautiful dress anyone could hope for, and all the trimmings. Whereupon her fairy godmother properly disappeared with a "pop" and the girl began to unpack all her lovelies. She called her friends to see, and as they were exclaiming, someone saw her poor limp homemade dress hanging on the door. "Oh **that**," she said. "It's something I tried to make myself. I could never wear **that**. It's a botch."

Now there are lots of things you can do for

yourself. But you cannot face God in your own "robe of righteousness." You must accept Christ and wear **His** robe of righteousness. And you cannot live a victorious Christian life in your own way, on your own strength, with your own abilities — be they ever so mighty. When Jesus said, "Without me, ye can do nothing," He meant it. You can go to church, yes, and be good, yes — but you cannot be the Christian He wants you to be, planned for you to be, **yearns** for you to be.

If you insist upon matching the notches and perforations of your own life, you will wind up in dismal failure after dismal failure — until you come at last to the point where you are willing to take Him at His word. He says, "abide in **Me** — and I in you . . . " There is your strength. There is your secret. And there is the power of your daily prayer time.

Abide in me, and I in you. . . . for without me ye can do nothing. (John 15:4,5)

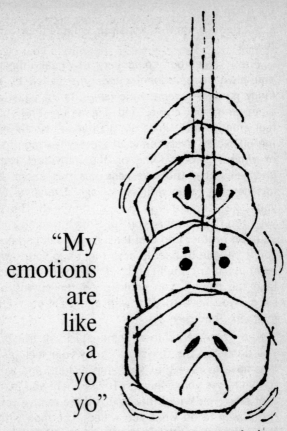

"My emotions are like a yo yo"

Naturally. Your glands are like a yo-yo. And as your glands go, so go your emotions. C. S. Lewis once said that the secret behind an apparently serene untroubled personality might be simply a good set of well-balanced glands and a good digestion. Well right now, your glands are in a turmoil, and to tell you to stop feeling the way you do is like telling you to stop bleeding and

27

expect you to turn it off, just like that. You just plain **can't.**

All right, if it's that hopeless, what is there left to do?

First, remember some very practical things. You have an emotional curve. It's called by a fancy name — cyclothymic curve, but it's just a plain emotional curve. And it goes up (and you feel great!) and it goes down (life isn't worth living) in cycles, every few weeks, every few months, or whatever, depending on the individual **you.** And remember that **everyone** has this curve. It has nothing to do with sex or age. Everyone. At your age your curve is curvier, that's all. But if you stop to think that your parents have one and your kid brother and that teacher you can't stand, you'll be able to handle both them and your own emotions more intelligently. If you really cared to take the trouble you could chart the curves of people you have to deal with and steel yourself for their "bad days."

And then remember some spiritual things. You don't live the Christian life by your feelings. You have to take that first step in faith and will to live above your feelings. The moment you take that step, you'll find that God is there to give you the power to do what you willed. The man with the withered hand had to stretch his hand out before it was healed. And as you cultivate this habit, you'll find your curves calming down. "I have set the Lord always before me: because he is at my right hand, I shall not be moved. . . . "

. . . I shall not be moved. (Ps. 16:8)

"He's
a nice person,
but . . ."

"He's a nice person, but . . . " and there you go again. If you hate yourself every time you do it, there's hope for you. If you reason that you are doing your Christian duty, watch out. You're in trouble.

There was a woman from the congregation of the famous Dr. Spurgeon in England, who went to him once with a complaint against another church member. She smacked her lips and after a preliminary "He's a nice person, but . . . " she proceeded to carve him up like a turkey, slice by slice. After she had her victim lying there with all the meat sliced off his carcass, she said primly, "The Lord has given me a talent for discerning the weaknesses in other people." "Madam," he said quietly, "THAT is a talent that I think the Lord would just as soon have you bury."

The Lord has plenty of things to say about judgment, as far as He is concerned. But He has only one thing to say about it as far as WE'RE concerned. DON'T. It's as simple as that. God is the **only** One who can judge. He says so repeatedly.

Before you start judging another, make a list of the pros and cons. That is only sensible. Put down the cons first. Why you should NOT judge. You cannot have friendship with God if you are in a critical mood. It will make you hard and unkind. It will make you feel smug spiritually, and that is OUT. God simply does not allow such nonsense. You will not help the person you are criticizing. You will only tear him down. But worst of all, you will be putting yourself on the spot, because every time you criticize, you condemn yourself. In Romans 2:1,2 it tells us " . . . for wherein thou judgest another, thou condemnest thyself; for thou that judgest doest the same things. But we are sure that the judgment of God is according to truth. . . . "

Now put down the pros. There aren't any. Not one. The Bible says so. Read Romans 2:1,2, again. Then go on to 3. And you'll see.

So if you are feeling critical about anyone, stop and take stock. There are circumstances in his behavior you know nothing about. Even if you think you know him well, there is always **one** thing you do not know about.

So resolve to be done with it. It won't be easy. It keeps coming back, that pesky little habit, like gnats flying about your face that won't brush away.

If nothing else works, remember what you are really like, when you're honest with yourself. That will hold you for awhile.

Judge not, that ye be not judged. (Matt. 7:1)

30

"But there's practically no harm in this at all"

There were a couple of characters in Bunyan's "Pilgrim's Progress" who fell into the trap. Their names were Christian and Hopeful, and they were walking along the King's Highway, following their guidebook (the Word of God) when they spotted a delightful little stile that led over the fence and into a meadow. And what a meadow! Grass like a putting green, a little brook, flowers and shade — birds and butterflies — it looked perfect!

"Let's go over," said Christian. "But it takes us off the road" — Hopeful was not too sure. "But," said Christian, it goes right alongside the main highway as far as you can see — and it looks like ever so much more fun." So they scrambled over the stile.

It did seem harmless enough. And it was very

pleasant. Just as pleasant as it had looked, and more so.

After they'd walked along awhile the meadow veered a bit, just slightly off course, very subtly. They did not notice. They were too happy. Then the grass began to get tough and sparse. The brook had disappeared sometime before. There were no more birds or butterflies. And they began to stumble over stones at first, then rocks. They did not notice. They were too busy. Then the sun went down and it got dark — and great pits began to appear and it began to rain. Then they noticed. They were way off course and the pleasant meadow had turned into something dreadful and it was dark and the way was dangerous and they were frightened and wanted to go back — but it was too late. They could not find their way.

Whatever idea you might be flirting with, if it takes you off the main highway it is not harmless no matter how harmless it looks.

If you have any doubts about doing it—DON'T. For as surely as God's in heaven, the picture will subtly change . . . and you'll find your pleasant meadow is a trap. "There is a way that seemeth right . . . but the end therein is death . . ."

Where's your yardstick? It's in the word of God. " . . . for the ways of the Lord are right . . . " (Hos. 14:9). "The statutes of the Lord are right . . . " (Ps. 19:8). "I have led thee in right paths" (Prov. 4:11).

Yes, there IS a way that "seemeth right unto man, but the end thereof is death."

There is a way that seemeth right. . . (Prov. 16:25)

"But this time I'm lower than I've ever been before . . ."

Well it may be just a mood, and it may be for a very good reason. And it's no good when elders say, "Nonsense, you're too young to feel like that." It is wearing to be told you are too young, as if it were a disease. The fact is, you do feel like that and it's very, very real. Indeed, your emotions are probably more intense right now in your teens, than they will ever be again. But pick yourself up!

In Bunyan's tale of "Pilgrim's Progress," Christian and Hopeful strayed into Bypath Meadow, and it was inevitable, of course, that they should get into trouble. They stumbled into the yard of Giant Despair and were subsequently seized by the old rascal himself and thrown into the dungeon of despair in his castle cellar. And there they languished, beyond all hope of escape. In fact their host poked his nose in one morning and suggested that they do away with them-selves, as they'd never get out. And he left them to think it over.

"He's right," said Christian. "We're licked. It is absolutely hopeless." And then he thought—"Wait a minute. Every day we've been here, we've spent the time batting our heads against the wall and feeling sorry for ourselves. Why haven't we asked God to deliver us? D'you suppose it's too late?"

Well, it was worth a try. And try they did. All through the night they knelt in prayer. And instead of despairing, they thanked God for being faithful, though **they** were not. They asked His forgiveness for grumbling and for their self-pity. And they began to **praise** Him.

It was then that Christian felt the key in his pocket. It was the key of promise. "Call upon ME in the day of trouble; I will deliver thee." He seized the key with a shout, and tried it in the dungeon door. The great door slowly creaked on its hinges and swung open! They were free.

It is odd that when we are in the dungeon, the last thing we think of is praising God. It just isn't the natural thing to do, and we always want to "do what comes naturally." It is, however, the "spiritual" thing to do—and it is exactly what God is waiting for you to do. Do it. Then pick yourself up! "I will deliver thee . . . and thou shalt glorify me!"

. . . I will deliver thee, and thou shalt glorify me.
(Ps. 50:15)

"But I've
already done it . . .
What now?"

If you are already in Bypath Meadow—get back on the King's Highway at all cost. It may be simple—it may be costly and difficult, depending on how deeply you are involved. The cost may be the ending of a friendship, the giving up of a habit, the loss of prestige in your school group, the giving up of something that is really very pleasant to you. Whatever the cost is, pay it. You are not in a pleasant meadow. You are in a trap.

Christian and Hopeful got back, finally, but after much difficulty. But oh how glad they were

35

when they finally scrambled back onto the King's Highway! Their troubles were over!

Well—not quite over. They hadn't gone very far down the highway when they saw two shining ones coming toward them. And as they came closer they saw that the shining ones carried golden whips. And then they thought they might be in for it. They were right.

They had to lie down alongside the highway and take a whipping. But according to Bunyan, they did not mind the pain for they knew that they richly deserved it.

Now God may punish you in the way you think of punishment—or He may not. He deals with each of His children in different ways. In Hebrews 12:6 we are told that "For whom the Lord loveth He chasteneth . . . "

Your own remorse may be punishment enough. Whichever way it turns out, however, remember to "despise not thou the chastening of the Lord, nor faint when thou art rebuked of Him" (Heb. 12:5). And then go on to verse 6 again. "For whom the Lord loveth He chasteneth . . . "

For whom the Lord loveth he chasteneth. (Heb. 12:6)

"But

the problem

is

still there"

You gave your despair to God and you thanked Him for being faithful and you asked His forgiveness for your grumbling and self-pity and just as He promised, the despair was gone and you were free to walk out of the dungeon but— the problem is still there.

It is still there and you had a sneaking hope that it would miraculously vanish. It is true that God did work in your heart and it suddenly does not look as frightening as it did—but why oh why didn't it go **away?**

Well, perhaps that is not what God intended. He does not promise that it will vanish if you pray; He promises to change your attitude from despair to determination and to give you the strength to face it. He does not say "as thy **wishes** so shall thy strength be." He says "as thy **days** so shall thy strength be." And that promise will meet your needs whatever you have to face. If there are others involved in that problem you will be better able to face them. Or you may find that your parents are not the ogres they seemed to be after all—that they will be anxious, eager to stand by you and that you will work it out somehow, together.

If the problem still remains, then that is the way God intended it to be. You will learn from it. You will be stronger for it. You will be a humbler and better person after you are finally done with it. Somehow—though you can't see it now, you will benefit from it in the end. For God has promised that all things . . . "ALL things, work together for **good** to them that love God, . . . to them who are the called according to His purpose . . ."

. . . As thy days, so shall thy strength be. (Deut. 33:25)

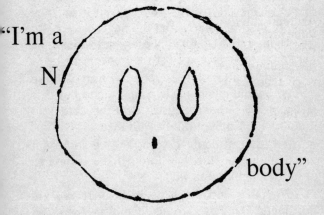

"I'm a N body"

So was Gideon, in the Old Testament. It was strange, when you stopped to think of it, that God chose Gideon. For Gideon wasn't a powerful man in any sense of the word. He wasn't the sort of man who could "win friends and influence people" at all. He wasn't even a particularly brave man. He was just a younger brother in a large family, and his father had the doubtful distinction of being an idol worshiper—he had a grove up on a hill with an idol of Baal and an altar! No, Gideon was anything but a picture of a hero. He was just a country bumpkin. If anyone had called him a mighty man he would have looked behind him to see if they didn't mean someone else!

But someone did call him a mighty man. And guess where he was when it happened? Hiding behind the wine press, threshing wheat! Yes he was, for those were the days when the Israelites were hiding in the mountains from their enemies.

So he was in a most ridiculous and humiliating position when he heard the voice. It was the angel of the Lord. "The Lord is with thee, thou mighty man of valor." And the angel went on to tell Gideon that God had chosen him to lead the Israelites to victory against their enemies!

Gideon sputtered, " . . . wherewith shall I save Israel? behold my family is poor . . . and I am the least in my father's house." And the Lord said unto him, "Surely, I will be with thee . . . "

Well, Gideon doubted then, and he kept right on doubting all the way through the campaign until the victory was won.

Are you a nobody? It could be that you are fortunate. For those are the kind of persons God likes to use. "I will be with thee," He says. And that makes you somebody! "For when I am weak (by myself) then am I strong (in Christ)."

> . . . for when I am weak, then am I strong.
> (II Cor. 12:10)

Boy

meets

girl

There is no end to the cleverness in novelty gadgets. They're strictly for fun, and most of them are meaningless. But once in awhile you do come across one that makes you stop and think.

There's one, for instance—two little figures, a boy and a girl. The idea is to put them on a table several inches apart. Then push them a little closer and—oops, they scurry toward each other with great haste until they've bumped heads, face to face. It's more fun to place them facing opposite directions and watch them turn around and smack into each other. The reason they do it of course is that each has a magnet glued against its face on the inside where you can't see it. One's positive, the other negative, and they attract each other. It's as simple as that.

And so it is with you. Boy meets girl. It's one of the steps in a long line of steps you take in this business of being independent. One of the first steps you took was to insist on feeding yourself, then saying "no" to everything your parents said "yes" to (you started this in your second year). And so on.

But one of the biggest steps comes when you struggle to get away from the companionship of adults in general, and your parents in particular. And you seek friends your own age.

And because God had marriage and children in mind when He made you, it's only a matter of time when these little magnets begin to operate and you find yourself irresistibly drawn to the opposite sex. Your problem is that marriage and children are a long way off in His plan for you, but the magnets are operating right now.

Well you can't just say "stop feeling." It doesn't work. But you **can** rest on God's promise. "There hath no temptation taken you but such as is common to man . . . " But, you say . . . this is different. It's hard to be faithful here. But listen. " . . . but **God** is faithful, who will not suffer you to be tempted above that ye are able; but will with the temptation also make a way to escape, that ye may be able to bear it." Believe Him! He will not let you down if you really mean business.

There hath no temptation taken you but such as is common to man . . . (I Cor. 10:13)

42

"I'm in tune . . . What's wrong with everybody else?"

Well, it IS discouraging. We go barging through life, doing our very best, getting our work done, obeying our superiors, even having daily devotions. What is wrong with everybody else? Why, in the name of common sense, can't they get along with us?

A very, VERY upset mother hauled her two teen-agers off to a psychologist once. She was

absolutely at her wits' end. She was a fine up-
standing Christian mother at that. Why couldn't
her children get along with her? "Give these
children tests," she cried to the doctor. "They
can't get along with me." But the doctor was
very wise.

"We'll all take tests," said he quietly. "What
do you mean, 'we'll all take tests?' " she said,
"they're the ones who need the tests." But the
doctor insisted. So they all took tests, and he
told them to come back in a week.

When they went back, he had their personali-
ties all laid out on graphs. Now you haven't lived
until you've seen your Christian personality laid
out on a graph. "Your son," said the doctor—
"he's okay." "Your daughter . . . " he continued,
"she's okay. Mrs. Smith, when can YOU come
back?" Mrs. Smith, it seemed, was a bit confused
as to who wasn't getting along with whom.

Now in all fairness to your parents, that situation could be, and all too often is, reversed.

Are people not getting along with you? And
you're in tune? Are you really? Ask yourself honestly who isn't getting along with whom. And ask
Him to show you if part of it is your fault. Then
face up to it, whatever it is. "If we say that we
have no sin, we deceive ourselves, and the truth
is not in us . . . "

. . . we deceive ourselves . . . (I John 1:8)

44

And . . . Peter . . . walked on the water, to go to Jesus. But when he saw the wind boisterous, he was afraid . . . (Matt. 14:29,30)

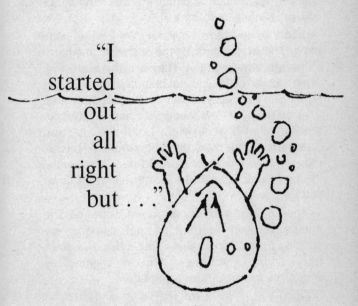

"I started out all right but . . ."

Well, where were the waves when Peter stepped out of the boat? Read the entire passage and you will see that they were there all the time. Way back in verse 24 it tells us—"But the ship was now in the midst of the sea, tossed with waves: for the wind was contrary."

When Peter first saw Jesus walking on the water, he cried out, "Lord, if it's really You—ask me to come to You on the water!" Well, when you pray a prayer like that, you'd better be ready for anything. Jesus called out, "Come." And Peter stepped out in blind faith.

But . . .

"When he saw the wind boisterous, he was afraid." He began to look about him and he did not like what he saw. The dangers . . . the obstacles . . . the actual circumstances. And so, of course, he began to sink.

Don't be too hard on Peter. We do the same thing. The circumstances, the obstacles, the hardships are always there. They are there already, when Jesus calls you to take a step in blind faith. But how easy it is to take that first step . . . or the first few steps . . . and THEN take stock of what is about you . . . all the "ifs" and "what ifs" and then the "oh, brother, this is rougher than I thought it would be." And finally, "I don't think I can make it after all." And down you go.

The minute you doubt, down you go. The minute you get to thinking that perhaps you shouldn't have done this thing after all, down you go. The minute you are overwhelmed by your circumstances, down you go.

Once you have heard His voice, and stepped out in faith, KEEP GOING. And if you start to sink for an instant, cry out as Peter did, "Lord help me!" And He will.

In verse 31 it tells us—"And IMMEDIATELY Jesus stretched forth his hand, and caught him."

And don't forget the rest of the verse. It is a gentle scolding. "Oh thou of little faith—wherefore didst thou doubt?"

"How
do I
keep going?"

How do I keep going—this thing that has happened to me does not just involve my today or my tomorrow or next week or even next month. It involves my whole future. I'm only in my teens but this thing is going to affect my whole life if it isn't solved at once.

There was a little boy in Scotland who wanted to be a doctor. All of his short life he'd dreamed of it, planned on it. One of the darkest days of his life was the day his mother had to take him out of school to help support the family. He had to go to work as an errand boy. There was nothing in life that could possibly have been more earth-shattering to that little boy than to be denied his education. There was a problem that was threatening to affect his entire life—everything he'd ever dreamed of.

Now he was probably not more than eight or ten years old—but he did something that would put many of us older Christians to shame. He did the most ordinary thing imaginable. He did the next thing that was set before him. He went to work as an errand boy. And he didn't go to work defeated, licked or resigned either. He went to work in complete trust, and left his problems with God. And he never doubted for a moment that God still knew what he wanted to be, that his life was in God's hands, and that the whole thing would somehow work out without his worrying about it.

How do you keep going? You simply do the next thing that has to be done. And leave your problem with God. That doesn't mean you simply sit back and let God do it. It means that you don't panic. Take the long-range view—do today's job, and in due time, when God is ready, He will show you how to work it out.

And the boy? Oh yes. He wrote a letter to God, reminding Him that He wanted to be a doctor, the postmaster gave it to his pastor and the church sent the boy back to school. You see?

Arise and build . . . (Nehemiah 2:20)

"But it's such a bore...."

It sure is. Dishes. Raking leaves. Cleaning your room. Emptying rubbish. It sure is. Well, here is where you have to just get up and begin, as if there were no God at all. Because if you wait until God inspires you, you will wait in vain. You surely won't see God in THIS thing if you wait all day. You've got to "arise, shine . . ." and take that first step.

"But it's against my nature," you say. Of course it is. It's against every teen-ager's nature no matter **what** he's going to be like when he's an adult. It just goes against the grain. Like

49

scraping a fork down a windowpane. It sets your very teeth on edge.

It is just wearisome drudgery. And drudgery is so far away from what you want to do, dream of doing as a Christian. Deeds of derring-do, yes —but this! Honestly.

Do you know what a touchstone is? It's a black stone, a cousin of flint, and it's used to test the purity of gold and silver by the streak left on it when it's rubbed by the metal. And we use the word to mean any test by which to test a thing's qualities.

Drudgery is a touchstone to test the quality of your character. Big crises are sometimes easier to meet. Your glands send out an extra shot of adrenalin and away you go. But the big tests don't come too often. Your quality of character is tested by the homely everyday routine. It is when you face up to drudgery that you find out if you're for real, as a Christian.

In John 13 you will find your Lord engaged in the most humbling kind of drudgery—washing the disciples' feet! And He said, "If I then, your Lord and Master, have washed your feet, ye also ought to wash one another's feet."

Arise . . . shine . . . and take that first step. And the moment you take it, you'll find that God was there all the time.

Arise, shine . . . (Isa. 60:1)

Cast thy burden upon the LORD . . . (Ps. 55:22)
For every man shall bear his own burden. (Gal. 6:5)

"Well,

which is it?"

Well, which is it? In one breath we are told to cast our burdens upon the Lord and He will bear them . . . and in the next we are told to bear our own. Which is it? It does seem a bit unreasonable.

Actually, both things are true, and they can both be true and still make sense.

There's the story of a man who had a burden . . . and it seemed more than he could bear. He came home very tired one night. He was carrying his burden in his heart. And he was carrying a package under his arm. And there, in the living room, was his crippled child in a wheel chair. "Where's mommie?" he asked. "Upstairs," said the child. "This package is for her," he said, "I'll run on up with it." Well, the child wanted to take it up and when he told her that was quite impossible she said, "No—it won't be hard at all. I'll carry the package and you can carry **me**!"

Well, that's how they worked it out. She carried the package and he carried her. It was simple. And as he was on his way up the stairs it struck him that his problem of carrying his burden was just as simple.

He would carry his burden all right, but the Lord would carry him! Suddenly his burden seemed lighter; he was not alone with it.

And that's the way it is with you. The Lord doesn't carry your burden . . . in other words, He doesn't always take it away. If He did, you would never toughen up. But He doesn't leave you alone with it either. No. You carry your burden, and He carries you, and right along with you He is carrying your burden also. "Blessed be the Lord who daily beareth our burdens" . . . and "Let every man bear his own burden" . . . are both true. You see, it all works out, after all.

Loneliness
is
not
being
alone

In "The Cross and the Switchblade" this preacher, who was doing a work among teen-age gangs in New York slums, asked one of the boys— "Angelo, what would you say was the greatest problem teen-agers have in this city?" "Lonesomeness," said Angelo quickly.

Now that was a switch. You would expect him to come out with just about anything but that. Loneliness in a city teeming with eight million people? Loneliness when these teen-agers were crowded into tenements with huge families? Lone-liness when there wasn't enough elbow room to move without bumping into someone?

Yes.

Webster says that loneliness is "without com-pany — lone — secluded from society — solitary." And indeed it is. But you can be without com-pany and solitary in the midst of a crowd, in the midst of your family, in the midst of even your friends.

Angelo knew that. And he said the feeling came because you felt that nobody loved you. That all his friends in his gang were really very lonely people. They ganged together in sheer desperation, and even then they were lonely.

Well these teen-agers had a far better reason than perhaps you do. For the truth was that no-body did love them nor cared what happened to them. And they did not know God, so there was no one, nothing, for them to cling to.

"But," you say, "I might seem to be better off but I'm not, really. Sometimes I feel that no-body does love me." You are probably wrong. Your parents may seem to be away off on the other side of an impassable gulf, impossible to reach or really talk to. But in about five years you will realize that they did love you all the time. Or you may be right. For the painful truth is, some parents **don't** care.

You need not be lonely, really. For in either case you have God's promise—"I am with you always."

. . . I am with you alway . . . (Matt. 28:20)

54

"My parents won't let me do anything"

Are you chafing under discipline? Your parents are too strict for your comfort? And you wail "All the others do it." Yes indeed. Well, of course it depends on who "All the others" are and whether it is really "all the others" or just a few and exactly what it is they're doing. In any case, let's just say you resent discipline in general. Webster says it means "teaching; instruction. Training which corrects, molds, strengthens, or perfects." It sounds hard to take, and it sometimes is.

The author of "The Cross and the Switchblade" lectured in Los Angeles and he said—and mind you, this was the fellow who went into the New York slums and took teen-agers whom nobody loved, the hopeless cases, and loved them right into the Kingdom of God—he said there should be a "woodshed revival" in the home to overcome the breakdown of discipline. He said that in his six years of work with narcotics addicts he had never met any who had had discipline in their homes.

"All the others are doing it?" Well, he went on to say that teen-agers have been given stock answers by their elders and yes, even by psychiatrists and other professionals to explain away their (and "their" means their elders) easygoing attitude toward sin. "And they haven't helped," he concluded. "All the others' parents are letting them do it?" Well, thank God your parents are not.

These poor teen-agers who are hooked on narcotics are there because they had no goals, no restrictions, no set of rules to live by, no "frame of reference" to stay inside of, no boundaries.

And when you have no restrictions it means only one thing. It means nobody here on earth really cares about you. God has commanded your parents to discipline you. "Correct thy son," He says, "and he shall give thee rest; yea, he shall give delight unto thy soul." In other words, he shall grow into adulthood being a responsible happy human being. Do your parents set boundaries for you? It may be rough to take. But just take God at His Word. And thank Him that they do!

Correct thy son . . . (Prov. 29:17)

More

about

discipline

But, you say, you are far away from the teenagers in the slums. Their problems are their problems. Yours are different. Let's bring it closer to home.

There was a very disgruntled letter in a newspaper "advice" column—there are many, but this was just one—that said: "My parents won't let me do anything the other kids do. Their strict attitude toward everything humiliates me in front of my friends. I have to be in by 11 o'clock and they want to know where I'm going and who I'll be with and everything. I'm in the ninth grade.

Isn't it about time I got to do what I want to do without answering to them for everything?" And it was signed "Embarrassed."

And a few weeks later another letter appeared in the same column. And it said: "This is an answer to "Embarrassed." Tell him or her to thank God for parents like that. My parents didn't care what I did. They didn't care where I was or who I was with. There was no law in our house—I just did as I pleased. And when I got into little scrapes they bailed me out and let me go on my merry way. Well now I'm in real trouble and there's no bailing me out. I wish my parents had cared enough to clamp down before it was too late." And it was signed "Embittered." In a survey of teen-agers who didn't have to sign their names, they admitted, practically 100 per cent that they secretly wanted discipline. They wanted to know how far they could go. They wanted boundaries to stay inside of. They wanted to know that somebody cared enough to discipline them.

And down in your heart you know that that is what you really want too. Or if you never thought about it before, think about it now. And thank God for parents who **care** who you're with and what time you come in! "For whom the Lord loveth He chasteneth . . ." It is also true of your parents.

For whom the Lord loveth he chasteneth . . .
(Heb. 12:6)

"I can't lick this habit"

Can't you? The author of "The Cross and the Switchblade" reports that of all the problems, of all the sins, of all the habits, of all the traps these teen-agers in the slums fell into, drug addiction was the worst. It wasn't only a "body" habit, it was a "mind" habit. You could lick the "body" part of it, after a few days of torture. But the mind!

Something in your mind kept telling you to go back to it. It was like a demon whispering to you, urging you. They called it "monkey on your back." And you just had to go back to the habit, no matter what your resolutions.

And yet he is able to report that of 300 narcotics addicts started through his program in six years, 80 per cent have been freed of the habit to the point that their desire for narcotics had gone. And forty of them are studying for the ministry!

Why? How could they lick a habit like this? and he says simply, "The Holy Spirit." But you say—that's all right for him to talk about. But the Holy Spirit is too much for me to get hold of. I'm only a teen-ager.

But these teen-agers "got hold of" the Holy Spirit. They knew Him as a Comforter, sent to them from God. They knew Him as a person, very real in their lives. They knew Him as the One Whom God sent to them to give them power over their problems and their habits. They were desperate. And they took this great promise, grabbed it, clung to it for their very lives. And it worked! And some of these teen-agers were only thirteen years old!

If they could do it to lick the most gripping habit known to man, you can do it with your habit, whatever it is. Claim the power of the Holy Spirit of God in your life. Right now. "And I will put my Spirit within you, and cause you to walk in my statutes, and ye shall keep my judgments, and do them . . ."

And I will put my spirit within you . . . (Eze. 36:27)

"How long
does
it go on?"

Discipline? Well, that's okay for little children. But I'm a teen-ager; I'm headed for adulthood; I'm right on the doorstep of being grown up!

Of course.

There was a young man once who was working on a farm for the summer. The hours were long and the work was hard. But the real point was, he needn't have been doing that kind of hard work. He needn't have been working at all. For his father was Calvin Coolidge, the President of the United States! He could have been back in Washington, or in Palm Springs, or in Miami, enjoying himself. That's exactly what one of his companions on the farm thought. "Why," said this companion "in the name of common sense are you here? If my father were president I'd be off somewhere having a good time."

And Young Coolidge said simply, "You don't know my father."

Well. Apparently this father was a man of high ideals and of principle. And the fact that he was president didn't alter his views one whit. He still believed that discipline and good healthful hard work were the things that would mold his son into the kind of stuff that would make him a man.

That's okay for little children? Well, this young man was in his late teens and he was still being molded. And what's more, he took it with good grace.

Do you have to work on Saturdays? And in the summer? Take heart. Read the biography of any person who really cut a swath in history and you will find that he worked like crazy while other kids were running wild.

God has put **your** parents in charge of **you,** for better or for worse. And they are the way they are, and you are the way you are, for a reason. Just thank God for them.

And don't be impatient. Mother won't sew name labels on your clothes when you go on your honeymoon. She'll let you go in time. Meanwhile . . . "Obey your parents in the Lord . . . for this is good."

Children, obey your parents in the Lord . . .
(Eph. 6:1)

There is a lad here, which hath five barley loaves and two small fishes . . . (John 6:9)

"But
what
can
I
do?"

What can you do indeed? You are just a teenager. And your days are most ordinary . . . nothing special happens. You'd be willing to go out and do something great; you'd be willing to go out and do something daring; you'd welcome the opportunity to do something brave and dangerous—but nothing comes up.

And so you go on about your daily round. It's rough. And you don't feel that you are accomplishing anything really great for the Lord. And that's exactly the way it was with our hero. Do you suppose that lad started out thinking that he was going to have a part in something great? Of course not. It was just an ordinary day. Like any other day. His mother packed him a lunch and off he went. And that was that.

As the day went on, he found himself in perfectly ordinary circumstances, nothing unusual. There they were, and it was lunch time, and so he got out his lunch and that was that. Nothing dramatic, nothing unusual. And then the opportunity came, suddenly, unexpected, out of the blue. There was an emergency. And he found himself saying—"I have five barley loaves and two fishes—"

Well, it was ridiculous. Five barley loaves and two fishes. And there were thousands of people there, hungry. But he'd burst out with it and now he was stuck with it, for whatever it was worth. But look what happened. They brought him to the Lord with his little bit of stuff, and the Lord took it and multiplied it until all those thousands were fed—out of his little piddling offering!

Your little offering? Take it to the Lord. He can multiply it a thousandfold, beyond anything you can possibly dream of!

"Well
here
it
is . . .
What
now?"

So you've brought your little offering . . . your "five barley loaves and two fishes" to the Lord.

It works. It works every time. But not always in the way you might think.

There was a woman, once, who went to the powers-that-be in Vacation Bible School. "Look," she said, "I have no particular talent. But I want to contribute. Even if I just cut out paper birds, well then, I shall cut out paper birds. Just so I can help." Now this woman had a secular radio program and had a "gift-of-gab" already. But somehow she never associated that gift with the

Lord. And, during Vacation Bible School, lo and behold, she discovered that she could tell stories the children would listen to—and so she dropped her secular work and went on to tell stories to children—and adults—and then to give lectures all over the world—and all because she had offered her little piddling offering for what it was worth.

Of course, it doesn't always work out that way. There was another woman who offered her talents, for what they were worth, to the same cause. And she did not go on to give lectures all over the world, but she did go on to raise a Christian family and to make an adoring husband happy, which was probably more important. Who can tell which woman did the most?

The point is, both of them offered their little offering—insignificant as it was—in all good faith, for the cause of Jesus Christ. And He multiplied each of those offerings in His own way.

It is not for you to say just **how** He will choose to multiply your little offering. Just give it. Give it, not caring where it goes. Just so long as He can use it. That's the point. "Surely blessing I will bless thee, and multiplying I will multiply thee . . ."

. . . I will multiply thee. (Heb. 6:14)

"But
God doesn't
answer
right away"

Doesn't He?

Back in the early 1800's, there lived a man who didn't get his prayers answered right away either. His name was Stephen Paxon. Steve prayed that God would take away his stammer when he was a little boy. When he was a man, he still stammered. But he hadn't spent his time moping in the meanwhile. He'd taught himself to read, to sing, and had established himself in a profitable business. When he started his Sunday School ministry he asked God again to take away the stammer. But it was four long years before he discovered that by breathing a certain way he finally had it conquered!

That was a long time to wait for a prayer to

be answered. But while Steve was waiting, he was too busy to sulk. Busy developing himself in every possible way, busy using his talents to the utmost of his ability, busy making the most of what he had. The long years of waiting had tested his metal, rubbed off the sharp edges in his personality, taught him patience, so that when the answer came he was ready for it.

If God doesn't answer you right away it is not because He did not hear or doesn't care. And it is not necessarily that His answer is "no." It may be "wait." What you are asking for may be something you are just not ready for yet. There are things to learn, preparations to make, talents to develop, character to strengthen.

There is much that He wants to do for you, and He must do it in His own time. And when, finally, your prayer is answered, you will be ready. And looking back, you'll be glad it was not answered when you wanted it, for you will see then that it would not have been right.

Read the whole verse: "And it shall come to pass that before they call, I will answer: and while they are yet speaking, I will hear." No matter how long the answer is delayed . . . or if the answer is "no"—you know He hears. And He cares.

. . . I will answer . . . (Isa. 65:24)

"Give
God
my
weakness?"

Are you adventurous enough to give your greatest weakness to God? The life of a Christian **is** an adventurous one, you know. It's full of surprises. God challenges you to take your greatest weakness and just give it to Him so He can show you what He can do with it.

It is easy to dedicate your talents. Your musical ability, your speaking ability, your keen mind, your leadership ability, your strong body. If you have made up your mind to follow Him, those are the very first things you want to turn over. But your weakness! **That** you want to hide! You even have a sneaking hope that perhaps God, after all, does not even know about it.

As fascinating as Steve Paxon's whole story is, the most amazing part comes at the very end. For after his great missionary work was established and others were able to take his place in the field, his job was to travel back east to Boston, New York, Philadelphia—all the key cities—and, of all things—speak! Yes, his final mission in life was to be a speaker! And as he told huge audiences about the Sunday School work, they sat listening—their very hair on end—he held them spellbound! And the hard-bitten newspaper reporters of those big cities were unanimous in their enthusiasm. Never before had they heard such a speaker. "He hypnotizes an audience," they wrote. "He has a manner of delivery that compels you to listen—and a voice like a silver trumpet." All his clippings were rave notices. The whole back of his biography is full of them. In the end, his speaking ability was his greatest strength.

The Christian life is an adventurous one. It's full of surprises. God challenges you to give Him your greatest weakness so He can show you what He can do with it. It could just possibly be, in your own life, that He wants to turn it into your greatest strength.

. . . For my strength is made perfect . . . (II Cor. 12:9)

"But my handicaps
are not physical"

Steve Paxon was a boy who stammered so badly he could not even blurt his name out on his first day of school. And so he was sent back home again—the teacher couldn't be bothered with him. As if that were not bad enough, he limped, too. So he was shifted about from place to place—nobody wanted him. He was apparently destined to be a total loss—licked before he even started.

But he took stock of his handicaps, and found out a number of very interesting things about himself. First, he could teach himself to read by asking people what the letters were on signs and in newspapers. And slowly and painfully he put the letters together until he was able to recognize the simpler words. Second, when he was a teen-ager, he discovered that he could sing. He had a golden voice, and what's more, when he sang, somehow he didn't stammer! And the limp? Well, he just decided to put up with it.

So he took what he had, such as it was, and went on to build the best possible life he could manage. And what a life it turned out to be! He wound up establishing 1300 Sunday Schools in the Mississippi valley—which was then pretty wild country. And on record, as a result of his work, 84,000 children were introduced to the living God.

Perhaps you don't stammer or limp, actually. You are strong and healthy. But your stammer and your limp are in your personality. Your wit isn't sharp. You don't seem to be able to communicate. You can't get your ideas across. You're tongue-tied when you get with the crowd. You can't enter in. You get embarrassed easily over your slightest mistake. Well, take what you have —such as it is—and give it to God and go on to build the life He has planned for you. God knows you through and through—every stammer, every limp. And He will show you things about yourself, traits you have, talents you have, that you never even knew existed!

Trust Him. You will find that He has really made you a much nicer person than you ever realized. "Thou knowest my downsitting and mine uprising, thou understandest my thought afar off . . . "

. . . Thou hast searched me, and known me. (Ps. 139:1)

"But I am only a teen-ager"

John Ring was a teen-ager too—a very ordinary one. He had no particular talents and no particular influence. He was about 15, a rookie soldier in the Civil War, and the aide to Captain Russell Conwell. His duties were to take care of the captain's uniforms, polish the captain's boots, and polish a very special dress sword the captain prized.

But the hardest thing he had to do had nothing to do with army duties. It had to do with his witness as a Christian. He had to read his Bible every night. He had to read it in front of Conwell. And he had to risk Conwell's friendship in doing so. For Conwell did not believe in God.

Now fighting an honest-to-real battle with bullets would probably have been easier, for Conwell was John Ring's hero, and it is hard to risk making a fool of yourself in front of your hero. But John Ring saw what God wanted him to do, and he did it. He did it night after night, first in the face of gentle scoldings and finally in the face of a real scorcher that would have curled the hair of most teen-agers and put them to rout. But John knew that he had to speak then or forever hold his peace. And he said, "Captain Conwell, I love you. You're the finest man I've ever known. But you're going to hell because you don't believe the most important thing that God has said." And he proceeded to give his captain the message.

The awful part of the whole thing was that it didn't seem to do any good. The message was not taken, John was squelched and that seemed to be that.

The message was to "take" some time later, though, for God intended to bless His Word. He did not intend to let John's witness be in vain. In the end Conwell not only capitulated to God, but went into the ministry!

You're only a teen-ager? Your witness could have far-reaching effects beyond anything you dare dream. God could cause you to be a spiritual giant in the life of another! "Let no man despise thy youth: but be thou an **example** of the believers, in word, in conversation, in charity, in spirit, in faith, in purity . . . "

Let no man despise thy youth . . . (I Tim. 4:12)

"I've got
all my life
to witne$s$$s$$n$$n$...

Everything that John Ring did for the Lord he did when he was a teen-ager. He had to. For he never lived to grow into adult life.

Not many weeks after he had witnessed to his captain, he had his chance to see some real fighting. Conwell was away on business when his company was surprised by the enemy, out of the blue one morning. They were completely disorganized and unprepared, and there was nothing to do but run. So run they did, across a wooden trestle bridge, in desperate haste to get to the other side of the river and burn the bridge behind them. Well they got over all right and set the bridge afire all right—but then John Ring remembered something. It was not a pleasant task, but he felt that he had to do it.

And he did.

He ran back across that bridge, grabbed the

precious sword from the center-post of the tent, and started back for the other side again. Before he had gone very far he was a flaming torch and they shouted at him to jump into the water, but he kept on running. He made it to the other side all right and the sword was safe. But he had paid a terrible price. For that night he went into the shining beyond and when Conwell came back, John was gone.

It was then that Conwell turned to God. He took the sword in his hand and leaned against a tree and prayed—"God, if you are real—reveal yourself to me. I must find John Ring's Saviour. I must find his Lord."

God took him at his word. Mission accomplished. And at a terrible price.

John did not witness to his captain because he knew he was going to die. He witnessed because it was the immediate job at hand to do for his Lord. He did not save the sword with any intention of dying. It was done in a moment of abandonment, a pouring out without thought of self, for a friend. But God used it to accomplish marvelous things and start Conwell on a great ministry. John did not know it, but it was the last chance he had.

You have your life ahead to witness? Probably. But God wants you to live your life for Him **now** as if it were the last chance you had.

Read the rest of the verse. " . . . And they that were **ready** went in with him to the marriage: and the door was shut."

. . . and they that were ready . . . (Matt. 25:10)

"I
can't
seem
to
work
up
any
steam .
: "

Enthusiasm is not something you "work up." It is something God has to give you. And you won't get it unless you ask for it.

After John Ring died saving his captain's prized sword, Russell Conwell was probably the most enthusiastic man for God in his generation. He went up to Philadelphia, built the great Baptist Temple, the largest Protestant church in the world at that time, the Temple University, the Temple Hospital, and while he was resting, preached with enthusiasm all over the country. The man was a dynamo. If you shook hands with him it was like putting your hand on a live wire. He oozed enthusiasm, he radiated it, like electricity. Everyone wanted to be near him; God had taken his personality and made it irresistible. And when people said to him—"You have enough enthusiasm for two men—what is your secret?" He said promptly, "The Holy Spirit of God." And then he always added—"but I have a human secret too. I have a sword hanging over my bed. And every morning I kneel by my bed and I ask, 'Lord, give me enough enthusiasm for two people today—myself and John Ring.' And every night I kneel there and I say—'John, I did two jobs today, one for myself and one for John Ring.' "

Now Conwell had a very good reason for asking enthusiasm. He owed a debt to John Ring that he could never really repay. But the point is, he **did** have to ask for it. God-given enthusiasm is just what it says. It is **God**-given.

Anything else you work up on your own steam will fizzle out sooner or later, and you'll find yourself dull toward the things of God, the edges blunted, your mind and your will lazy.

Now you don't have anything as dramatic as John Ring as a reason to ask for it. But you do have a reason every bit as important. God has apprehended you, "gotten hold of you" for a purpose. And if you are ever going to "get hold" of this purpose God wants you to do it with enthusiasm. Just think what He could do with just one enthusiastic teen-ager! Purpose in your heart that you will be that one!

Whatsoever thy hand findeth to do, do it with thy might . . . (Ecc. 9:10)

"What has God done for me?"

What did God do for you when He saved you? In order to understand it, it's necessary to look in on this word "justice" and think about it.

Justice is "merited reward or punishment." In other words, when you get justice—you get (if you'll forgive a lowly pun, and it will be the only one in this book) "justice" you deserve—one way or the other.

There is a legend about a king who was very noble and very wise. But above all, he was just. Now at the time of this legend, his people were very wicked, and in order to stamp out the wickedness, he made a special law—and whoever was found guilty of breaking it would have both his eyes put out.

Well, someone did. And when he was brought

to the king—it turned out to be the King's own son. The whole court waited in breathless silence for the great king to pronounce sentence. And what this king said is something to think about. He said, "My son—I am your father and I love you. How can I be just and spare you from darkness? If I were only a king, I could punish and forget. If I were only a father I could forgive and forget. But I am a king **and** a father. I have made a law and you have broken it. The punishment for breaking this law is that two eyes be put out. And I hereby decree that two eyes **shall** be put out. One of yours—and one of my own."

And so it was done. And when the people saw, they said, "He is indeed a just king. How great and sacred is his law. He is a loving father, too. How great is his love!"

God has done more than that for you. He has taken upon Himself, not half, but **all** the punishment in the person of Jesus Christ. That is His justice.

What is God doing for you now? He is still dealing with you in utter justice—His laws must be upheld—but there is still Jesus Who took your punishment, and Who is ever there at the right hand of His Father, making intercession for you, pleading for you when you make a mistake. "If we confess our sins, He is faithful and **just** to forgive us our sins . . . " and to give us another chance.

The just LORD is in the midst thereof; he will not do iniquity . . . (Zeph. 3:5)

"I look a fright"

So you're not as good-looking as you hoped you'd be? You dreamed that you'd grow up like a fawn, graceful and lovely—a vision to look at? You dreamed you'd grow up like an Apollo— huge and well built and a delight to look at? And instead of all that, you are all awkward, with some extra fat that **won't** come off—or you're skinny and those muscles **won't** fill out— and your glands have gone berserk, producing too much oil and causing that wretched acne and all the rest of it?

Well, it **doesn't** seem fair. Some teen-agers go through adolescence like a breeze. Their glands behave and their skin stays nice and they somehow seem to escape that worst of all buga-boos—the "awkward age." And, let's face it, some don't. Those of us who do are indeed for-tunate. But let's take those of us who don't. And get down to some straight thinking.

The worst thing we can do is mope about it.

The better thing we can do is realize that there is good diet, exercise, discipline in health habits, good grooming, excellent helps on good taste in dress. With all the aids we have today in magazines and newspapers there is no excuse for anybody's being unattractive physically! Some of the most beautiful women in the world do not have regular features. Some of the most attractive men in the world are actually homely; they simply radiate the vitality of good health and a charming personality! So there's no excuse, really.

But the **best** thing we can do about it is to give ourselves to God. What, exactly **is** a "charming" personality? As a Christian, it is "God in you," working through you, giving you enthusiasm and vitality and the power of the Holy Spirit, so that you are actually "contagious"—you draw people to you like a magnet! And in some unaccountable way, you are attractive, no matter what your looks!

And, stop and think, perhaps the very fact that you are not "good-looking" is a blessing. For in the striving to be attractive as a Christian, you have more hurdles to get over, more difficulties to encounter, more physical problems to solve—and in the doing you will find that in some mysterious way God has made you more attractive than your more "physically endowed" companions. **You** may, in the end, be the fortunate one. For your attractiveness will never fade!

. . . *the LORD looketh on the heart.* (I Sam. 16:7)

82

"I wish I could be
my own boss"

So you would like to be your own boss. So would we all. "If I could be on my own I know I'd be happy." Dream on!

There's a story of a bee who got bit by that same bug of independence. He flew into somebody's house by mistake once, and the folk who lived there saw him on the window pane. And, for the purpose of the story, they began to discuss bees. Then he found out. He found out that he was a worker-bee, born to be under authority all his life, and would never be anything else. He flew back to the hive, mad as a hornet, and got his fellow-bees to rebel and fly out for themselves and establish their own colony. Well, they fell to quarreling over who would be boss, and got nowhere. In the thick of it, our little bee left in disgust, ran into an older bee, and decided to live with HIM. "Who'll be the boss?" asked the older bee. "Why YOU—you're the wiser." "And who'll be the worker?" asked the older bee. "Why ME—I'm the stronger." And then he saw right away how things stood. He was right back where he started from. So they both decided to go back to the hive and let the queen bee rule the roost, which was the way God had planned it.

Everybody answers to some authority. Nobody is, in the long run, his own boss.

When you stop answering to your elders, you will start answering to a boss, who is answering to a boss, who is answering to a boss, who is answering to the top boss in the outfit, who is answering to his power and money, for if he does not behave in a certain way he will lose both. And everybody, in the end, is answering to God.

"Let every soul"—that means you—"be subject unto"—that means placed under the power or dominion of another—"the higher powers." God tells us that in Romans 13:1.

"FOR—" He goes on to say, and this is the point—"There is no power but of God; the powers that be are ordained of God"—that means they were appointed by God . . . over you.

So what then?

He tells us "what then" in verse 2. "Whosoever therefore"—that means you again—"resisteth the power, resisteth the ordinance of God . . ."

It's as simple as that. If you resist the authority over you, you are resisting what God **appointed** over you. You are, in the end, resisting God.

And don't take it lying down with a "you can't win" attitude. Take it rejoicing. Just think. The One Who has the **final** authority over you is God, your Father, Who loves you—and Who wants the very best for your life. You can't beat that.

Let every soul be subject unto the higher powers.
(Rom. 13:1)

"My parents expect
too much"

And you're afraid you can never live up to what your parents expect of you? In a national survey of junior high and high school students this turned out to be the biggest bugaboo—the deepest fear of most teen-agers. That they couldn't be the "100% specimens" their parents apparently expected. And if you're a "PK" (a preacher's kid) it's worse than ever! What a great deal you have to live up to!

There is something to be said on both sides. Parents—and especially those parents in Christian work—sometimes **do** get unrealistic and carried away—and they place a burden on their children that is too great to bear. There was a father once, in Christian work, who took his son to a psychologist and cried—"Our hopes for him were that he would be a missionary—now he wants to be a school teacher." And after many hours of patient counseling, the psychologist said, "Accept him and love him—not for what you wanted him to be—but for what he **is**." It is a hard order. And hard medicine, sometimes, for parents to take.

There was another parent once, whose son came to her—and she was in Christian work—and said, "Mother, I want to be a farmer." And she wisely said, "Then be a good Christian farmer."

So your parents expect you to be something you're simply not up to? And they're making your life miserable? Well perhaps they **are** wrong. But wait a minute! That does not absolve **you** from all responsibility. Don't lose your head. And don't just give up and decide that if what is expected of you is too much, then you'll just give up and be **nothing**—it isn't worth the struggle. That's fatal, and totally unfair to you as a worthwhile person. And to what you **can** be, were **meant** to be.

Don't lose your heritage just because your

parents are unreasonable. Stop and think. What does **God** want you to be? Are you all right with **Him?** Ask Him, with all your heart, and whatever it is, don't be discouraged. He loves you. He has a purpose for your life. But don't go into a snit and throw it all down the drain in discouragement and rebellion, before He has a chance to work it out!

. . . and what doth the LORD require of thee, but to do justly, and to love mercy, and to walk humbly with thy God? (Micah 6:8)

"I hate to be
a poor sport"

There was a group of teen-agers once, many years ago—who gathered together in one of their homes for a party. They felt gay and carefree and a bit wicked too, for the parents had gone for the weekend and the sky was the limit. None of them had any idea of downright immorality, but they did have some beer and they did plan to assert their independence by having a ringing good time. As their tongues loosened and they got into the spirit of the thing, the jokes got more and more off-color and then someone started some songs that were not all they should be and the laughter got louder—

And then they noticed that someone was missing. "Where's Ginny?" someone cried. And everyone was quiet. "Oh, Ginny," their host said with a shrug—"she didn't like our jokes. She got Rob to take her home."

After an uneasy moment, everyone got to singing again, but something had happened. Somehow the songs had lost their flavor and the jokes seemed stupid and everything they were doing in their hectic attempt to have fun, seemed a bit shoddy. They made a **valiant** attempt to keep that party going strong; they really tried. But it was no go. The thing had been spoiled somehow, the thrill had gone, the evening had gone flat.

And though not one of them would admit it, they felt a little soiled, a little stupid. There was not one boy in that crowd who didn't secretly respect Ginny. And there was not one girl in that crowd who didn't hate Ginny for the moment, but who didn't secretly wish she had had the intestinal fortitude to have done what Ginny had done.

Ginny had decided to stand alone and let the chips fall where they may. Those teen-agers were not Christians; but Ginny had behaved in a manner to put some of us Christians to shame. It's something to think about.

Watch ye, stand fast in the faith, quit you like men, be strong. (I Cor. 16:13)

"What
does God
want
of me?"

Apprehend means to "get ahold of, to grasp, to capture." And it can also mean to "get ahold of" a thing with your mind, to grasp it, to understand it. You were "apprehended" by Christ. And He apprehended you for a purpose. Now He wants you to understand, to "get ahold of" that purpose. The pity of it is, too many Christians never do grasp the purpose for which Christ grasped them.

There was a couple in the Old Testament who wanted a son. And the angel of the Lord appeared to them and told them they would have that son, and that he was to be "set aside" for the Lord. So you see he was dedicated to the Lord's service before he was even born.

His name was Samson. And what a person he was! God had given him great strength and many talents. There was a great life ahead for him and God had a purpose for that life. But he went down in defeat at the end, his life a pitiful loss. And the reason was lust.

Now lust, in its broadest meaning is wanting something right **now.** "I Want What I Want When I Want It," the song goes, and that can mean **anything.**

You can bulldoze your way through life, impatient and selfish, getting what you want at any cost, and leaving a trail of trouble and broken hearts behind you in the doing.

And all God's plans for you, and all His purpose for your life will go down the drain because you failed to "get ahold" of it.

Our constant prayer must be that we "get ahold of" the purpose behind what is happening to us in life so that God can have His way with us.

And the time to do it is now. In your teens, while life is still ahead of you.

I follow after, if that I may apprehend that for which also I am apprehended of Christ Jesus. (Phil. 3:12)

"Can I
trust
God
in this?"

This crisis is big, this crisis is real. Things look so absolutely hopeless that I must work it out myself.

There was a man in the Old Testament who did that. His name was Elimelech, which means "God is My King." His crisis was real all right— there was a famine in the land. But instead of trusting God and staying in the land where God wanted him, he took his wife Naomi, and his two sons, and marched them off to Moab, where God most certainly did **not** want him. And there he died. And his two sons died. The rest of the story you know; it is in the book of Ruth.

But the interesting part about the beginning of this story is the meaning of the names. Elimelech means "My God is King." Naomi means "pleasure." The two sons' names mean "sickly" and "pining away." And the land of Moab means "desire." And when Naomi finally returned to her native land she said to her friends, "Call me not Naomi, call me 'Mara' "— which means "bitterness."

So Elimelech, whose very name meant putting God first in his life, married pleasure, went to the land of desire, the fruits of his life were sickly and pining away—and then he died and pleasure turned to bitterness.

What a dismal picture of a life! He did not "get ahold of" God's purpose for his life, because he did not trust God in a crisis.

There is no crisis in your life that God does not know about and that He cannot handle. "He shall direct thy path . . . " yes, but there's more to that verse. "In all thy ways acknowledge him, and He shall direct thy paths." And (Ps. 37:5) "Commit thy way unto the LORD; trust also in him; and He shall bring it to pass . . . "

. . . he shall direct thy paths. (Prov. 3:6)

"I won't get over this in a hurry"

You've been hurt. Someone you loved and trusted has hurt you and you're still smarting. And it's robbing you of your pleasure in prayer time and coming between you and all your good resolutions, so that everything in life is somehow colored by it and things aren't as much fun any more. Well, there's another fellow in the Old Testament who didn't "get ahold of" God's purpose for his life, and for this very reason. He couldn't forget his hurt feelings. His name was

Absalom. He had a little run-in with his father and had to flee from home. But though his father David could forgive and forget, Absalom could not. His one goal in life was to get even with his father. And years later, when he finally did march against his father, David's orders to his soldiers were "deal gently with Absalom"—but Absalom's only thought was to "get my father."

And so Absalom's life was a total loss, and the reason was bitterness.

One of the most damaging and costly emotions you can have is bitterness. It can ruin your personality, it can rob you of your looks, it can even make you ill, physically! So don't waste your teen years picking up fistfuls of thistles of bitterness.

One of the happiest habits you can cultivate is a good forgettery. Have you been hurt? Forget it. Today's **another** day God gave you, and by His grace, there's tomorrow ahead. So, " . . . forgetting those things which are behind, and reaching forth unto those things which are before, I press toward the mark for the prize of the high calling of God in Christ Jesus." Or, as Phillips puts it in modern translation, "I leave the past behind and with hands outstretched to whatever lies ahead—I go straight for the goal . . . "!

. . . forgetting those things which are behind . . .
(Phil. 3:13)

Is
jealousy
eating
you
?

Jealousy can do just that. Eat away at your very personality and leave you suspicious and petty—a thoroughly unlovely teen-ager.

One of the greatest characters in the Old Testament failed to "get ahold of" the purpose God had in his life and the reason was jealousy. His name was Saul, and God had given him just about everything a person could wish for. He was tall and handsome—he was rich and powerful—he was talented—he had everything to live for. And then along came David. And when David's winsome ways threatened Saul's popularity, Saul forgot all his own blessings and spent the rest of his life trying to ruin David. And in trying to ruin David's life, he wound up ruining his own. He went from the very top to the very bottom. His jealousy ate into his personality and changed it completely. It took him far from God. He began his life asking God's guidance in everything, and before his death we find him asking guidance of a fortune-teller!

Recognize jealousy for what it is. It is your cruelest enemy. Recognize it for what it does. It spoils you as a Christian and as a person.

If you are plagued by this rascal, run, don't walk, to God and ask Him to deal with it. He is the only one Who can help you; you cannot help yourself. For jealousy is against all reason, all logic; you cannot deal with it.

It is one monster you don't have to put up with, one problem you don't have to have.

. . . jealousy is cruel as the grave: the coals thereof are coals of fire, which hath a most vehement flame.
(Song of Solomon 8:6)

"But
I can't be thankful"

There are times, let's face it, when life looks so glum and things seem to be going so badly that for the life of you, you can't find one thing to thank God for. If you've run out of things to thank Him for, stop and seriously consider this matter of communication.

Have you ever thought to thank Him that you can communicate? Communication is the ability to explain to others who you are and what you mean. And it's the ability to understand others—who they are and what they mean. You do this by what you say, what you write, your smile, your laughter; you do this by seeing, listening, and reading. You can communicate by your moods and your feelings, without saying a word. How wonderful that God has given you this marvelous ability. And how easy it is to take it for granted.

There was a girl once, in a psychiatric ward, who gave the nurses no trouble at all. She simply sat where she was put, without moving, staring straight ahead. They actually had to change her position occasionally to stir up her circulation. You could light a match and pass it in front of her eyes, real close, and she would not even blink. Her case was a pathetic one. She had fallen into moral trouble, and her feeling of guilt was so overwhelming that she had crawled way down inside herself to a place where she could never be hurt again. She had completely withdrawn from the world. She was unable to communicate. She was only fourteen.

You could not look at her and ever take this matter of communication for granted again. That you can see and talk and write and read and hear and laugh! Or if you are lacking in one of these senses, God has made it up to you by giving you extra sharpness in the others. How wonderful!

If you once start to think about it, you'll be overwhelmed with gratitude. And you'll "let no corrupt communication proceed out of your mouth [or from your personality] . . . but that which is good . . ."

Let no corrupt communication proceed out of your mouth . . . (Eph. 4:29)

"I'll
pray
tomorrow"

In this business of communication, you try to tell others who you think you are and what you think you mean. But only God can help you understand who you really are and what you really mean. So it's a dangerous thing indeed to let your communications break down where God is concerned.

There was a plane ready to land, but it kept circling the field until the passengers became restless, wondering what the trouble was. The clouds were heavy, but they didn't seem to be that bad. Then the pilot's voice came over the speaker. "Ladies and gentlemen, you'll have to be patient with us for awhile. We will be unable to land until further notice. There's a small private plane lost somewhere in this area, and they're keeping the landing field clear until this plane can establish contact with the control tower."

A little plane with its radio conked out, and totally helpless to land in those clouds, without communication. The passengers waited. Then, after about twenty minutes, the big plane suddenly zoomed down for a landing. The pilot had made no further announcement. It had to be bad news, or he would have said something. Sure enough, on the news that evening was the report. The little plane had crashed. Without its communication system working it had lost its way and crashed.

Now, you can stop communicating with God and still live. You can go your own way. But it will not be the life He had planned for you, it will not be His best for you, it will be nothing compared with what you could have had if you had kept in touch with Him. He is your only reliable guide. He will never fail. He will never make a mistake. And He will help you understand who you are and what you mean, for no one knows you like He does.

. . . I . . . will tell thee all that is in thine heart.
(I Sam. 9:19)

Enthusiasm

is

contagious

In England, a father was as puzzled and be-wildered as parents all over the world, and for the same reason. It was his teen-age daughter's reaction to a popular singing group. "I just don't understand it," he said to her. "Why do you bother to go? You are all screaming so, you don't hear them anyway." "My **word,** Daddy," she said, "you don't go to **hear** them. You go to hear them to **scream.** If you want to **hear** them, you buy a record!''

Of course.

The idea is to have a cause, to have a hero, to have someone or something to adore, to have something to scream about, something to get excited about.

Can you imagine what could happen to the cause of Christianity if teen-agers were to get that excited about **it?** Not the screaming, of course, but the motive behind the screaming— intense enthusiasm. Enthusiasm is the spark that gets a thing done. Wherever teen-agers have been enthusiastic about Christ, they've lighted a great fire that could be seen all over the church and throughout the community. They've put their elders to shame, their pastor to shame, their parents to shame. For no one, but no one, can be as irresistibly contagious as an enthusiastic teen-ager.

Enthusiasm for Christ is not just something you drum up. Enthusiasm for Christ is something God **gives** you. Just as ''the love of God is shed abroad in our hearts by the Holy Spirit'' (Rom. 5:5), God will shed enthusiasm abroad in your heart if you ask Him. ''restore unto me the **joy** of thy salvation.''

Restore unto me the joy of thy salvation; and uphold me with thy free spirit. (Ps. 51:12)

"This thing ahead of me is too difficult"

And you don't think you're going to be able to face it. It looks dreadful there, staring at you from out of the future, like a monster in a nightmare.

In Bunyan's tale of "Pilgrim's Progress," one of the first things his hero, Christian, had to do was to climb the hill of difficulty. There was no other way to go, for his guidebook told him to keep going straight ahead, and there it was—straight ahead. Well, first he ran and then he walked and then he crawled, it was so steep. But he was determined to get to the top, for at the top was the Palace Beautiful, a place he'd been longing to get to.

Well, to make matters worse, halfway up he saw two men running down as if the devil were after them. As they flew past him they shouted, "There are lions up there!" which gave him quite a jolt, you may be sure.

He kept going without much enthusiasm, and the farther up the hill he got, the more frightened he became, with the thought of those monsters, staring at him from out of the future. Sure enough, when he reached the top, there was the Palace Beautiful off in the distance, and there were the two huge lions, one on each side of its gate. And they were roaring roars loud enough to chill the heart of the strongest Christian. He stood stock still, wondering whether to go on and face them or turn back, when he saw a porter in the doorway of the castle. The porter shouted something at him and gestured for him to come on but Christian couldn't hear what he said. "I can't hear you"—cried Christian—"those lions are making so much noise!" The porter shouted again—and this time Christian heard him. "The lions can't hurt you—they don't have any teeth!"

And sure enough, they did not. And when Christian got right up to them it turned out that they not only were toothless, but chained.

Which is the way it is with most of your prob-lems. They are toothless when you finally face them. Don't turn back. You'll miss the Palace Beautiful.

Is any thing too hard for the LORD? . . . (Gen. 18:14)

Your
secret
weapon

In Bunyan's tale, when Christian got inside the Palace Beautiful it was everything he'd hoped for and more. Discretion was there. And Prudence and Piety and Love. And he sat around with them and the other members of the household and they talked about their Lord and had communion. Then he slept in the room of peace.

The next morning, before he left, they took him to the armory of the palace to equip him for his journey. They equipped him from head to foot. They gave him the helmet of salvation, the breastplate of righteousness, the shield of faith, the sword of the spirit — and they shod his feet with preparation of the gospel of peace. He tried this outfit on and thanked them heartily, "for now I have everything I need to fight," he said. But they told him "no." There was one thing more. And this is what they did.

They led him down a corridor, and at the end of this corridor was a door. They opened the door and he looked inside the small room. There was nothing in it. "What's this?" he asked. And they told him it was the most important part of all his fighting equipment. It was his secret weapon. It was the closet of prayer.

It was a good thing he had it, too, for he had hardly gone a mile in his journey when he needed it desperately.

God commands you as a Christian to put on His whole armor. All of it. Salvation, preparation, faith, righteousness. The sword, which is your Bible. Truth.

For the Christian life is warfare, make no mistake about it. Satan has declared all-out war on you. And without your armor — and your secret weapon — you do not have a chance against him. "Pray to thy Father which is in secret" (Matt. 6:6).

Ephesians 6:14-18

Humiliation
hurts

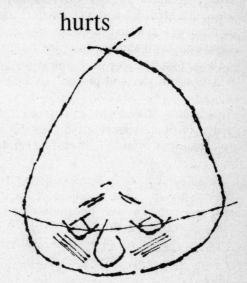

It was in the valley of humiliation that Christian needed that secret weapon so desperately. For it was in the valley of humiliation that he met Satan.

"Who are you?" cried Satan. And Christian told him he was a Christian, that he belonged to the Lord. "Oh no you don't," Satan said. "You are still mine!" And the battle that followed was terrible to see. Satan flung his darts at Christian, and as they flew around Christian's head, he heard whispers and horrible doubts—and he wondered if after all Satan were not perhaps right —if all this business of being a Christian was not nonsense after all—

It was then that he dropped his sword.

And it was then that Satan nearly finished him off. But, just in time, Christian remembered—his secret weapon! He used it desperately—and the whispers stopped and the doubts disappeared and he was able to grab his sword and he "resisted the devil and the devil fled from him."

It is in the valley of humiliation that Satan will come to you and plague you with doubts— doubts of your salvation—doubts of victory over sin—doubts of God's very existence. It is in the valley of humiliation that you will be your very weakest—that you will most desperately need that "secret weapon."

For humiliation weakens you and twists you inside. It hurts. It is unbelievably painful. When you are in that valley, remember—God is there. He put you there for some reason. And if you take His hand through it all, you will come out of it unharmed—and a stronger Christian for having been there.

Remember, after the armor in Ephesians 6:14- 17 comes verse 18. "Keep on praying in the Spirit, with every kind of prayer and entreaty at every opportunity, be ever on the alert. . . . " (Williams translation)

Praying always . . . (Ephesians 6:18)

Sin

is

attractive

One of the places Christian had to go through was Vanity Fair. And Bunyan didn't picture it as a horrible place at all. It was like a huge carnival, noisy and gay and very exciting. There were gaily decked booths everywhere, with hawkers shouting their wares—''Come buy lies, come buy cheating, come buy deceit!'' There were steaming bowls of pottage, there was immorality of all descriptions and wine and what's more, they all looked attractive. Bunyan tells us that Christian looked not to the right nor the left, but kept his eyes straight ahead and replied, "I buy nothing but the truth." According to Bunyan's tale, the people of Vanity Fair made things very tough for him and he barely escaped. But somehow he managed to, though the going was not easy.

Sin **is** attractive. If it were not we wouldn't be tempted; there would be no fight at all. The Christian life would be easy.

"But how do I know what is sin and what is not?" It's a good question. If you are right with God, you'll know. For He has given you a guide; the Holy Spirit. So when the Holy Spirit whispers to you and there's that familiar little twinge in your conscience—**don't.** Or, if you are in doubt about the thing—**don't.**

Is there anything left that's fun? Yes. "God has given us richly all things to enjoy." Is there any fellowship that can equal that of a group of happy Christians? Is there any laughter as hearty or contagious? Once God has "gotten ahold" of you, you are His—and you'll never **really** be happy again without Him.

. . . God, who giveth us richly all things to enjoy.
(I Tim. 6:17)

Are you
a spiritual snob?

Of course, if you are, you'll be the last one to know it. And if you are, you are in a very dangerous position.

In Bunyan's tale, Christian and his friend Hopeful went through thick and thin together. The way was hard but they were happy, for they'd put up a good fight and their problems had only made them stronger. They had the satisfaction that comes from doing a good job. As they got stronger the way became easier; the lessons they had learned had made them wise, and the unpleasant skirmishes grew fewer and fewer as they learned the secret of victory in their lives.

Things were really going well for them. The road was easy and the problems few.

And then suddenly they realized that something was wrong. Nothing they could put their finger on—just a vague sort of—well, you might call it drowsiness. As they looked at each other and yawned, they realized that it **was** drowsiness. Then they noticed something. There were poppies growing along the side of the road. Then they noticed something else. There were other Christians alongside the road too. And they were sleeping. Then they realized where they were.

"This is the Enchanted Land," cried Christian. "The place our guidebook warns us about. The place where Christians get so smug they fall asleep!" Sure enough, it was. The land of the poppies.

Satan will never give up on you. If he can't get you any other way he will inject the thought into your mind—"By jove, but I'm spiritual." And there he has you. By the roadside, sleeping.

What did Christian and Hopeful do about it? They began to talk about their salvation and in the talking they began to get grateful all over again, and the old excitement, the old joy, the old enthusiasm came back. "Restore unto me the joy of Thy salvation. . . . " Are you a bit smug? Watch out.

Wherefore let him that thinketh he standeth take heed lest he fall. (I Cor. 10:12)

"I'll do it, Lord, but I know it's hopeless"

These verses contain quite a story—a story full of questions. Jesus was in Peter's boat, just off-shore, and he was teaching the crowd that had gathered on the shore to listen. After He finished, He turned to Peter and said, "Launch out into the deep and let down your nets for a draught" (of fish). Now Peter was a seasoned fisherman. He knew his business. And at the moment he apparently felt that Jesus didn't know what He was talking about. "Lord," said Peter patiently,

"We have fished all night without catching anything. But if you say so . . ."

And so it is with us. "Lord," we cry, "the situation is hopeless. But if you say so . . ."

Well, Peter and his companions let down a net. The question is, why didn't they let down the other nets? Jesus had said, "nets." But Peter had thought—"Oh well, I'll let down one, anyhow." And he did.

And then he got the surprise of his life. The net was no sooner in the water than it was filled with fish—so filled, in fact, that it began to break under the load. And they had to call to their partners in the other boat to come help them. There were enough fish to nearly sink **both** boats.

Then Peter knelt in worship before the Lord, for—and this is the part that is hard to believe—he was astonished! And so were they all. Why, in the name of common sense should they be astonished! Wasn't Jesus the Lord of the impossible?

Well, we know it too, but we pray to Him and when He tells us what to do, we do it halfheartedly (**one** net) and then when He answers above and beyond anything we had ever dreamed, we are astonished! Lord, help us to believe He can do anything, obey Him wholeheartedly (**all** the nets) and expect the impossible.

I will . . . show thee great and mighty things.
                                              (Jer. 33:3)

You are
now becoming
what you
are going to be

On the rear wall of a college auditorium is a plaque. It's there for the students to see as they leave the auditorium; it's there for the speakers on the platform to stare at. It's there to make everyone who sees it slightly uncomfortable. It says: "You are what you have been becoming." Now **that's** something to make you stop and think! If you're older, it can make you squirm. If you're a teen-ager, it can give you hope. For if you turn the thing around and juggle it a bit, it follows logically that you are "still becoming what you are going to be."

You're not suddenly going to become a great

Christian when you are older, when it's convenient, when you suddenly make up your mind. Nobody develops a strong character overnight. It's done over a long period of time. What you become as a Christian and as a person depends to a large extent on the decisions you are making right now.

Fanny Crosby became one of the greatest hymn writers of her day. But that was a long time after she made her first decision for God. That first decision happened when she was eight years old, right after she had found out that her blindness could never be cured, that she would live out her life in darkness. She got alone with God, and she told Him quietly "I won't mind being blind, Lord—if you'll just give me a job to do. Give me a job to do, and I'll do it with all my heart." And she put away her self-pity and got on with the business at hand, leaving her future with God.

The most important decisions in life you are making right now, as a teen-ager. Everything you are going to be, you are now becoming. And the more you give Him of yourself right now, the more He can do with you—and through you—and **for** you. "Remember now thy creator in the days of thy youth . . . while the evil days come not, nor the years draw nigh, when thou shalt say, I have no pleasure in them. . . . "

Remember now thy Creator in the days of thy youth . . .
(Ecc. 12:1)

What do you want from God?

When Fanny Crosby was eight years old she made a decision that affected her whole life. And then she wrote this poem to her grandfather:

"Oh what a happy child I am,
　Although I cannot see . . .
I have resolved that in this world
　Contented I will be
So many blessings I enjoy
　That other people don't.
So sigh or cry because I'm blind?
　I cannot—and I won't!"

And as she grew into her teens, she never forgot that decision. She didn't ask God—"God, I won't mind being blind if You will only make me smart. Or make some wonderful man fall in love with me. Or help me to be rich. Or popular. Or famous. Or let me have the clothes I want." She didn't even ask for an important job. Just a job of God's choosing, and she'd tackle it with all her heart.

And God gave her what she asked for, and more. He opened the way for her to go to a school for the blind in New York—He gave her a wonderful mind—she graduated from college in three years with the highest marks in her class— she became a famous hymn writer—she was popular. And as if that weren't enough, the "most wonderful guy in the world" fell in love with her and she had a lovely romance and the happiest and most blissful of marriages. And as if **that** weren't enough, she became so famous and adored that she was invited to Congress to speak, and received a standing ovation and a standing invitation to return! She knew every bigwig in Washington by name, and counted as her close friends people who went down in history. And all because she asked God for a job!

What do you want of God? Something for yourself? Or a job of His choosing? If your wants are right, He will see that you get them, and then He will go on to do that "exceeding abundantly above all that you can ask or think. . . . "

Now unto him that is able to do exceeding abundantly above all that we ask or think . . . (Eph. 3:20)

Licking

the big ones

doesn't

just happen

King David was "becoming what he was going to be" when he was a teen-ager. He didn't kill that giant out of the blue. He was a long time working up to it. And he was prepared.

He was prepared spiritually by long hours alone with God while he was watching his sheep on the hillside. He was prepared physically by good living and hard work . . . so that when a lion attacked his sheep he was able to kill it. He was prepared talent-wise, too. He was a whizz with a sling long before that giant appeared. He had practiced with wild animals that threatened his flock. Once when a bear attacked his sheep he reached for his sling, took careful aim, and with devastating accuracy hit that bear a stunning blow, right between the eyes, felling him. His eye was keen, his body was strong and healthy, his aim was sure, long before he ever saw Goliath.

So when the big test came, he was up to it. He took his staff and his sling. He carefully selected his stones, put one in his sling and walked toward what was, up to that moment, the biggest problem he had ever faced. And the problem didn't run away. It stayed right there and dared him. "Am I a dog—" shrieked Goliath, "that you come to me with a staff? Come over here and I'll give your flesh to the beasts."

But David ran, with the grace born of training, toward his problem shouting—"You come to me with a sword—but I come to you in the name of the God you've defied! He will deliver you into my hands—that all the earth may know there's a God in Israel" And his stone found its mark and his problem fell before him. He was prepared.

The problems you're facing right now are the lions and the bears. They're for you to practice on, to grow strong on, so that when the giants loom on the horizon, you will be prepared. Physically strong. Mentally keen. And spiritually ready, from time alone with God.

"Prepare your hearts unto the LORD and serve Him only: and He will deliver you out of the hand of the Philistines."

. . . prepare your hearts unto the LORD . . .
(I Sam. 7:3)

"I want to be a good Christian —

But
my
parents!"

If you expect your parents to accept and love you for what you **are**—not what they expected you to be—then, in all fairness, you have got to do the same with them.

Are they breaking down everything you wanted to believe in by preaching one thing and living another? Are they short-tempered? Well, stop and think.

Did you ever—have you ever **once**—stopped to think of them as **people**? As people who went through the very same teen-age maelstrom as you are going through—who had hopes and dreams—who planned big things and perhaps got stuck with little things instead—who are worried over money and health and personality problems and a million little things that you have never dreamed of? Have you ever stopped to think how much they loved you as a baby, how they doted and exulted over your first steps, your first word, your first sign of intelligence? Or how they planned for you, hoped for you? And then somehow, in the confusion of life, they settled down to being just people on a treadmill, and perhaps they seem to have lost something. And they're not quite living up to what you expected.

Or are they perfection personified, but just not understanding? Do you find it hard to talk with them? Be encouraged. At teen-age, there is a great gulf between you and adults and it is for a very healthy and sound reason. You've **got** to grow up, that's all there is to it, and somewhere in the growing, you've **got** to establish somehow your independence. And in establishing it, you feel the compulsion to break away—to cut the psychological umbilical cord, to be "on your own." And so you stop talking to your parents.

Well, it's a great and mysterious paradox. God knows you have to establish your independence, but He still insists that you "honor thy father and thy mother." And for a reason.

He gave them charge over you. And you can grow up, establish your independence, and **still** listen to them. Accept them as they **are**—not as some impossible ideal you'd dreamed of. Listen to them. For they have the wisdom of experience. They know, because they've learned the hard way, through all their mistakes.

Ask God today to help you accept them as **people.** And, if they are amiss—don't condemn them, hands down. **Pray** for them! And in praying that God may change **their** attitudes—He may wind up changing **yours.**

. . . pray one for another . . . (James 5:16)

Are
you
for
real?

"Lovest thou Me?"

God asked Peter that question. And Peter, in effect, replied—"Lord You **know** that I do. I have spoken up for all Your ideals. . . . "

Well, God is asking you. And you reply, "Lord, you **know** that I do. I have spoken up in young people's meetings, I have worked hard for Your cause, I have upheld all Your ideals . . . "

But Jesus asked Peter again—"Lovest thou Me?" And Peter replied—"Lord, Thou knowest I do"—and he meant—"I have been in the company of those who loved You—I have left all my old friends—"

And God is asking you. And you reply—"Lord,

you **know** that I do. I have left all my old friends, my old pleasures—"

But Jesus asked Peter again. "Lovest thou Me?" And Peter replied—"Lord, Thou knowest I do—I have dedicated my life to serve Thee—"

And God is asking you. And you reply—"Lord, You **know** that I do. I am serving Thee in young people's meetings and in all the activities of the church—"

So you have. You have upheld all His ideals— you are in the company of those who love Him— you are serving Him—

But He is not asking you if you uphold His ideals, or if you are in the company of those who love him or if you are serving Him—

He is asking you, simply, if you love Him.

Have you ever stopped to think about it?

Jesus Christ, the creator of the Universe, the living God—asks you if you love Him!

And that is what He wants from you. To love Him.

Think of it!

Is it easier to just uphold His ideals? Easier to be in the company of those who love Him? Easier to serve Him?

Well, you can't just conjure up this kind of love. And God knows you can't. You ask Him to give it to you. "Because the love of God is shed abroad in our hearts by the Holy Ghost, which is given unto us . . . "

It is a gift.

. . . lovest thou me? . . . (John 21:15,16,17)

"Does God answer specific prayers?"

Well, He's no Santa Claus. Let's get that straight right now.

There was an old man, once, in Scotland (and this is a true story). And he was very poor. Well, it seems that he wanted to go to a series of evangelistic meetings in a nearby town. And because he was poor, he had to walk. On the way he stopped to eat a bag lunch he'd packed. And after he had given thanks for lunch he remembered something. "And, Lord," he said, "I need a front seat in those meetings, for I'm sorta deaf. And I need shoes. Mine are 'most worn out. And I need a place to stay." And he thanked the Lord in simple faith, and went on his way.

Well, when he got there, the place was crowded. And as he was standing in the back of the church, his hand cupped to his ear, an usher came up to him. "I beg your pardon," said the usher—"but would you follow me?" So the old man followed him—right up to a front seat alongside a young lady. She turned to him and whispered—"My father told me, if he couldn't make it, to give his seat to some worthy person.

I saw you standing there—your hand cupped to your ear . . . " The first prayer was answered.

Then, when they prayed—he knelt and she stood—you could have your choice in those days —and she saw the holes in the soles of his shoes. When they were seated again, she whispered— "My father owns a shoe factory. My coachman has a key—would you accept a pair of shoes as a gift from the Lord?" The second prayer was answered.

And after they'd stopped at the factory and got the shoes, she said, "Now I'll drop you off wherever you're going." And he said, "Well, I don't know exactly where I'm going. My Father promised me a place—but He hasn't told me where it is yet." "Your father? " she said. And then she said—"Oh—you mean God." Yes, he meant God. And then she said, "Please—there's an extra room at our house. Won't you please —as from the Lord?" The third prayer was answered.

And the old man spent a week of heaven, listening to the meetings, and having all his needs cared for.

But it just so happened that what he asked for was exactly what he needed—not what he wanted, but what he **needed**—and what the Lord intended him to have, if he would only ask for it.

Does God answer specific prayers? Yes. But don't expect Him to be a Santa Claus. It depends on what you're asking for!

. . . for your Father knoweth what things ye have need of, before ye ask him . . . (Matt. 6:8)

Does God answer specific prayers?

Yes. But it depends upon what you're praying for. In "The Cross and the Switchblade"—this country preacher asked himself a question. "What would happen if I gave up TV and devoted those two hours (the late show) to prayer?" And the next thing he did was put out "a fleece." He said, "Lord, I'm going to put my TV up for sale tomorrow morning. And if you really want me to do this thing, have it sold, send a buyer right away—within a half hour after the paper appears on the streets."

Well, that was **some** fleece!

But, do you know that the next day, within one minute before that half hour was over, the phone rang. It was a buyer. And he wanted the TV set, sight unseen, and said he'd pick it up in fifteen minutes!

Well, that was an answer!

It was an answer that took this country preacher into hours of prayer instead of TV—that took him into the slums of New York to help crime-soaked teen-agers, that took him into fantastic adventures of faith, that took him into a ministry that resulted in the salvation and rehabilitation of hundreds of teen-age dope addicts, that took him into paths he had never dreamed of, and all because he had taken one adventure of faith, asked God for something specific, almost a dare, you might say, and when God had answered, he had acted upon it.

Well, he acted upon it every step of the way, and he got the most fantastic answers to prayer you ever imagined—they were unbelievable they were almost like a fairy tale, something out of this world. Everything he asked for he got. And everything he asked for that he didn't get, it turned out wasn't right.

Yes, God answers specific prayers. If you're asking in faith, in the Holy Spirit, if you're asking because you really want His will in your life.

. . . let your requests be made known unto God.
(Phil. 4:6)

It's a mad, mad, mad, mad world

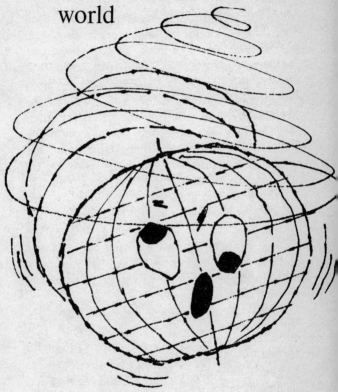

Yes, and you live in it. You were born into it and you are condemned to live in it. In one of our contemporary books it is said—"It is amazing, how an idea can rest undisturbed in the mind of people, for centuries, giving confidence, and then suddenly emerge one morning as a haunting question that threatens one's life with utter confusion. And now, right where we're living, is such a morning." And then it goes on to say—"We might want to believe otherwise, but the truth is that ours is a generation of intense confusion . . . "

Well. This is the age you were born in. Face it. You, as an intelligent teen-ager, know it. You read the headlines. You know the probable score. It is indeed, a "mad mad mad mad world."

Esther thought so. She was born into a world of utter confusion. Her people had not only been invaded—they were in danger of losing their identity—their very existence. Now it's one thing to read the headlines and think these things are so, and it's another thing to be responsible for their solution. She, it turned out, was responsible. You know the story.

What did she do? Well, at first, as a young person, she did not want to do anything. She was secure, a favorite of the king, her life was set—why should she risk all her present prosperity and guarantee of love and security and go stick her neck out?

But her cousin Mordecai said, "Perhaps you were born into the kingdom for just such a purpose." And then she really stopped and thought.

Why was she born indeed? For herself? Or for God's purpose? It was quite a decision. And you know the story; she faced the king, risked her life, saved her people. . . .

Why were you born? And why were you born into this mad mad mad mad world? The answer is—

You were born into this world for "just such a purpose." To do His will, come what may. You were born into . . . "and now, where we're living is just such a morning . . . "

You. **You** were born into . . . and for a reason. Ask God what it is. He is still in command. Ask Him what, as a young person, as a teen-ager, what He wants you to do . . .

. . . who knoweth whether thou art come to the kingdom for such a time as this? (Esther 4:14)

"My prayers
for other people's
salvation
don't
seem to count"

There was a man once who did not believe in God, and he made a great point of it. He was a scoffer, loud and clear.

Well, some Christian acquaintances of his began to pray for him. Every time they happened to be together and there was prayer, they included him in it. But there was one man in this group who decided to go one step further. So after one of these sessions, he got his horse and buggy and drove to the man's house. "I just want you to know that I'm concerned about you. And that I'm praying for your salvation. And that I cannot bear for you to be lost." And he rode away.

Well, now, that was a stopper. And it stopped the scoffer in his tracks. He went to his friends and he said, "Here's a new twist. This fellow came to see me. And he didn't argue. He never said a word except, ' . . . and I cannot bear for you to be lost.' " And then tears unaccountably began to run down his cheeks. "Oh, that guy," he said, "I couldn't argue with him . . . I can't answer him. I can't make it out. I've never cared for **him,** but he drove five miles today because he cared for me." Then he began to think that it was about time that he should be concerned too. And it wasn't long before he was knocking at "that guy's" door asking him what he must do to get right with God.

Your prayers for others' salvation don't seem to count? Well put some teeth in them. It was this man's **concern** for the scoffer that really counted. God could have saved the scoffer without any help. And He can save those on your prayer list without any help. But He **wants** help —from you. If your prayers and your arguments aren't doing any good—try **concern.** And you will find your power in witnessing greater than you had ever dared dream!

. . . *yet have I made myself servant unto all, that I might gain the more. (I Cor. 9:19)*

"I would
do it, Lord
but
I know
it's impossible"

Do you remember the pool of Bethesda? (Read John 5:2-9.) People who had serious physical handicaps lay around it, day after day, waiting for a chance to be healed. For at certain times, an angel went to the pool and "troubled the water," and whoever first stepped in was healed.

Well, there was this man who'd been apparently flat on his back for 38 years. Day after day he waited there. But there never was anyone to carry him to the pool in time.

Now here was a man who certainly wanted something. Otherwise he would not have been there in the first place. But when his prayer was finally about to be answered—when he came face to face with Almighty God, Who could, and was ready to give him what he wanted, he began to consider all the human reasons why it could not be done. "You see," he reasoned, "I've been trying this thing for years, and it is just no use. I've given up hope. I would do what You ask, but I know it's **impossible!**"

Well, Jesus didn't reason with the man. He didn't preach. He didn't remind him of how powerful God was. And He didn't coax. He simply said, "Get up." And it's to the man's credit—that he finally saw the light—and he **got** up.

Well, what are you waiting for? You have access to the same God. You want to have victory over this thing—you want to be rid of it once and for all? And God is telling you that you can and you are saying—"But God, You see I've been struggling with this thing and I'm just a teenager and I know it's quite hopeless. In fact it's **impossible.**"

Don't expect Him to take that for an answer. He will only tell you to "get up, and get going." So don't say, "I would do it, Lord, but it's impossible." He is offering you victory over this thing. Take it. But, to take it, you've got to get **up.**

John 5:2-9

"I have more troubles than anybody"

Do you?

There's a legend about an old fellow called Time, who delivered a package to every new-born baby. And with strict orders that everyone had to carry those packages through life and, sooner or later, open them. The rich babies got beautifully wrapped packages and the poor ones got theirs in plain brown paper—but inside, the contents were all the same. They contained the "troubles of life."

Now, of course, nobody liked what was in the packages and naturally nobody wanted to carry them. But they wouldn't burn and they wouldn't sink and there seemed to be no way to get rid of them—So, in the end, they all had to carry them along the journey of life. But the interesting part of the legend is the various ways people carried those packages.

Some of them opened them, took one look—and tied them all up again. Then with a long string they tied the package around their necks so that they hung down in front. Of course, they were very heavy, so the people who carried them that way were all bent over, their heads down, missing all the beauty and seeing nothing but the ground.

God intended you to have problems, but that is not the way He intended you to walk with them. And if you do choose to walk that way you are missing the whole point and the package, on you, is wasted. For the package was meant for your **good.**

The legend goes on to say that a kind fellow named Experience suggested that these bent-over people put their troubles behind them. Which they did, and of course the weight of the package straightened them up with such force that they walked with heads erect, eyes uplifted —so that people looked at them in wonder that they could bear their burdens with such grace.

"But He knoweth the way that I take; when He hath tried me, I shall come forth as gold."

. . . when he hath tried me . . . (Job 23:10)

Stumbling stones

In the legend of the packages, the interesting part was the various ways people carried them. Some people opened them, took out the troubles and spread them along the road of life. And then they proceeded to stumble over them. When they reached the end of their journey they were bruised and sore and of no value to anybody because they had stumbled over what had never been intended as stumbling-stones at all.

But there were others who spread them along the road and stepped up on **top** of every trouble that came their way. And so they made stepping-stones of what they found in their packages.

Which is what God intends you to do. "Happy is the man whom God correcteth; therefore despise not thou the chastening of the Almighty." Why? Because your problems may be blessings in disguise. He may have put a difficult person in your life to make you patient. He may have allowed you to make that mistake in order to shame you into being less critical of others. You may have to share that room or those possessions in order to be made less selfish. The thing that irks you the most could be the very thing that is going to do you the most good.

Instead of getting bruised on your problems, determine to turn them to your advantage. Ask God what He wants you to learn from them. The moment you use them as stepping-stones, the sharp edges seem to be gone.

. . . happy is the man whom God correcteth . . .
(Job 5:17)

The

choice

is

yours

There seemed to be no end to the ways in which you could carry those packages of trouble Father Time had left.

The legend goes on to say that you could take out a problem at a time, examine it at great length, then tie it around your neck so you could see it. And show it to all your friends. And discuss it endlessly, until all your friends and relatives got utterly weary and worn out looking at and hearing about that problem. You could do this until you became such a crashing bore and a burden both to your friends and to yourself, that people would hide when they saw you coming. Your problems would become **millstones.**

Or, you could take a problem, one at a time and put it by the roadside to mark an event in your life. Then when you looked back on the road you had come along you could see all that you had passed by that you would never have to pass again. It made your problems beautiful **milestones.**

You may have no choice in that problem that is irking you right now, but you do have a choice in how you handle it. It is no sin to talk it over with a trusted friend. One of the most wonderful blessings God has given us is friendship. And one of the most beautiful things about friendship is that we can share both our joys and our sorrows. But this kind of sharing can be one of the most abused blessings in the book. Discuss your problems, yes, but not endlessly and not in every conversation. Even your dearest friends will grow weary.

And when you talk those problems over with God, remember that they are actually working **for** you if you handle them the way He wants you to. "For our light affliction, which is but for a moment, worketh for us a far more exceeding and eternal weight of glory. . . . "

For our light affliction, which is but for a moment . . .
(II Cor. 4:17)

"I hate to stand against the crowd"

Well, there was a man once who hated to stand against the crowd. But he did. His name was Micaiah. He appeared in history for one brief moment and disappeared, never to be heard of again. Let's see what he did. And let's see what happened. Meet the man, who, with all the odds against him, knew he was on the winning side. It's quite a story.

The wicked King Ahab wanted to march against an enemy, and he called all his "yes" men and asked them if he would be successful.

And as "yes" men always do, of course they said "yes."

Now there was one man who was very unpopular among the Godless ones. An unimportant prophet named Micaiah. "But," cried Ahab, "I don't want to ask **him**. He never says what I want him to." But he was finally persuaded to call for Micaiah.

Well, Micaiah was on a spot. He had a choice to make. And he made it. "As the Lord lives, I will speak what the Lord speaks to me."

And he did. He prophesied Ahab's doom. And what did he get for his trouble? He was put in prison on bread and water.

It turned out, of course, that he had been right. Ahab **was** doomed. The battle was lost and he was killed. And what happened to Micaiah? The Bible doesn't tell us. He just disappeared into nothingness. Never to be heard from again. But he had stood up against a king and 400 prophets . . . and dared to speak the truth for God. The people may have forgotten him. But you may be sure God had not. He is with God right now and some day you will meet him.

You hate to stand against the crowd? Listen, when you are on God's side, you're a winner. You may not be carried around on shoulders and cheered, but you **can't lose.**

You have God's truth. Even if you're alone with it, the only one with it, like Micaiah—don't ever be afraid to tell it.

For they loved the praise of men more than the praise of God. (John 12:43)

"I want a new thrill"

There was an old junk dealer once. He was tired of his old routine. He was tired of his old ways. And he was tired of his old horse, Clemmy. And one day he decided to ditch it all. He didn't know exactly when the idea had first come to him—somewhere along the way when he felt he was missing life and he suddenly felt stale and defeated. Was that when it had burst upon him that Clemmy was dull, tired, mangy? He didn't exactly know. He only knew that suddenly—he decided to ditch it all, get rid of Clemmy—and start something new.

And so he did. He sold Clemmy down the line, and ordered a new horse. "I know just the one for you," cried the dealer. "A wonderful horse—new, exciting—I can get her here for you to-night." And the old junk dealer fell for it.

As soon as he'd left, the dealer gave orders. "Take Clemmy," he cried, "and give her a clipping, a shampoo, a manicure, dye-job — the works!"

And so Clemmy got the works. And when the old junk dealer called for his new horse that night he saw a beauty, smooth as satin. He was delighted. He paid his bill and started for home, and just driving down the street with his new beauty was a wonderful adventure.

And then something happened.

Unaccountably, he began to miss Clemmy. He began to think about how happy he'd been with Clemmy, after all—and how **right** they'd been for each other.

And while he was missing Clemmy and lamenting his impetuous new choice, this new horse clopped without guidance up and down all the right streets toward home. And before he realized what was going on, the new horse clopped right into his own driveway and into his own barn.

Then he knew. It **was** Clemmy!

The old man was unbelievably happy. What a narrow escape he'd had! But for the dishonesty of the dealer, he would have lost his dearest friend.

You might not be so fortunate. If your old routine seems dull, think carefully before you "ditch" it. The new thrill has a price tag on it and the price may be more than you care to pay.

So before you decide to find a new thrill, ask God to help you look at your old routine with new eyes, with a new attitude. For, if you are right with God, the Christian life is never dull!

If you want a new thrill, "sing unto the Lord a new song." And He'll show you great and wonderful things, with your new attitude.

Sing unto the LORD a new song . . . (Isa. 42:10)

"What does prayer time mean to me?"

Well, what DOES your prayer time mean to you? What did you expect to get out of it? And what, exactly, **are** you getting out of it?

There's a fascinating story, written by John Bunyan, about a town called Mansoul. And in the very center of Mansoul was a beautiful castle. In this castle lived a prince who ruled over Mansoul with love and justice. Indeed He loved Mansoul more than life itself. Now the most important people in Mansoul were Lord Will and Mayor Understanding and Mr. Conscience. And, being important people, they had many privileges. But one of the most precious privileges they had was this. Every morning they got up and went to the door of the beautiful castle and knocked. And they were let in to see the prince. And there, in the banquet hall of the great castle, was a table spread with the most exquisite delicacies —the most wonderful food they had ever seen. It was strange food—quite unlike any they were used to—it was food sent especially from the kingdom of the prince's father. Well, they sat at this table with the prince, and they ate to their heart's content. And after the feast was over, they just sat around and talked with the prince. They didn't talk AT the prince—they talked WITH him. They asked him all sorts of questions, and they listened while he answered. They told him their problems and they listened to his advice. They told him their disappointments and they listened to his comforting words. And they listened while he told them all sorts of wonderful things—things they'd never dreamed of before.

The time flew so quickly they scarcely realized where it went. And those visits to the castle became so precious as time went on, that they could hardly wait to get back there again. Those visits became the most important part of their lives.

Now Mansoul, of course, is you. And the Prince is none other than Jesus Christ Himself, in your heart, in the very center of your personality. And those "important people" in Mansoul are the most important parts of your personality—your will, your understanding, your conscience. And the most precious privilege you have as a Christian is to go to Him in quiet each day and sit at the table He has prepared especially for you. To go to Him and eat the strange and wonderful food which is the Word of God.

What does your prayer time mean to you? It means fellowship with the living God! That's what He wants it to mean to you. For that's the way He planned it. Tell Him you love Him. Tell Him of your hopes, your disappointments, your failures. Ask Him questions.

But **listen** to Him, too!

And there I will meet with thee, and I will commune with thee . . . (Exod. 25:22)

"What does
the Holy Spirit
mean
to me?"

In that tale of Bunyan's, there was another at the table during those morning feasts. When Prince Emanuel had first come to rule over Mansoul, he had brought with him a very important person. And when he introduced this person to the people of Mansoul he had said, "He is from my Father's court—dictator of all His laws. He will be your chief teacher, your highest guide. Oh, I want you to love Him as you love me. For He is the same in honor and power as my Father and Myself. Indeed, He is the very spirit of my Father."

What does the Holy Spirit mean to you? It is important for you to decide right now whether the Holy Spirit is a person to you or just some sort of "force" or "power." If He is not a person, to you, then you are robbing Him of your love and your worship. And you are getting robbed of a very important part of your Christian life.

When Jesus left the disciples he promised to leave them a "comforter." (John 15:26) And He told them—"when the Comforter is come . . ." and He didn't say "it"—He said "HE shall testify of me." In other words, "He will tell you that I am a fact. I'm real."

And later on, in John 16:13, he said, "When He . . . is come, He will guide you into all truth: for he shall not speak of himself." . . . and in verse 14—"He shall glorify ME."

That's why you know so little of the Holy Spirit. He never speaks of himself. He was left here to speak of Jesus. To make Jesus real to you. To comfort you. To guide you into truth. To teach you. To give you power over sin and over yourself and your weaknesses.

The moment you believe that He is indeed, a PERSON—He will become as real to you as Jesus is. God the Father is the judge. God the Son is Jesus, Who took that judgment upon Himself so you could go free. And God the Holy Spirit is the One Who will give you power to live your Christian life.

What does the Holy Spirit mean to you? Ask God, right now, to make Him real to you, so that you will know that He is a PERSON. Don't leave Him out of your life.

. . . he will guide you into all truth . . . (John 16:13)

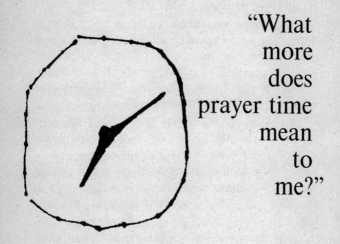

"What
more
does
prayer time
mean
to
me?"

Well, it would seem that Will and Understanding and Conscience would have had enough in that banquet hall each morning. Strange and wonderful food, the companionship of the prince and the lord high secretary—strange and wonderful tales — their questions answered — yes, more than enough. But there was something more.

For when they left, the prince gave them gifts —precious jewels—gold chains—dainties—things they'd never imagined or dreamed of. He pressed them into their hands and closed their hands over them—for they were secret things, for them alone.

There are so many things about yourself you can't explain to other people. Even those closest to you. Even people your own age. You can talk and talk and TALK but there's an ancient Chinese poem that goes:

"There's no use in talking—
   "And there's no end of talking—
      "For there's no end of things in the heart."

How true.

There's no end of the things in YOUR heart. And no matter how you tried to get them all out or explore them or try to understand them or try to make some one else understand them— you would never even scratch the surface.

But you can talk to God. For even if you do not understand yourself He understands you. And even if you cannot make others understand you, He knows you through and through. Before you even speak, He knows the thoughts in your inner-most being.

There are secrets you can share with God. Secret hopes and fears and ambitions and de-sires and struggles you would never dream of telling anyone else.

And, strange as it may seem, there are some things God shows you and tells you in your prayer time that you would also never dream of telling anyone else. They are yours and yours alone to treasure. Those are the secret gifts—the precious jewels—the gold chains—the dainties He presses into your hand and closes your hand over them—they are to keep for yourself. Just between you and God. How wonderful to have a friend like that!

What more does your prayer time mean to you? It can mean more than you can ever hope or dream. For He is able to do "exceeding abundantly above all that we ask . . . or think." (Eph. 3:20)

And I will give thee the treasures of darkness, and hidden riches of secret places . . . (Isa. 45:3)

"My prayer time has become a duty"

For awhile everything was going well. But now something is wrong. And now you are in the depths of discouragement. It just didn't work. And you cry, "Why . . . why . . . WHY . . . am I such a dope?"

Don't be discouraged. You are at the end of a long, long line. Listen to some more of Bunyan's tale. "Yes, those were golden days. Peace and harmony were everywhere. The friendship of the lord chief secretary (The Holy Spirit) gave them joy and power that they'd never known before. It was in the air like a sweet perfume. And that lasted all that summer. . . . "

BUT

Something happened!

What?

Well, all sorts of things can happen. But listen to what happened in Mansoul. . . . First, listen to what the prince had told them. . . . "Watch and pray," he had told them . . . "do not deceive yourselves . . ." And of course. The last thing they wanted to do was to deceive themselves. Spoil all that happiness and prosperity? But, well . . . it was hard to tell who was an enemy and who was not . . . Take this fellow, Mr. Carnal-Security, for instance. . . .

Mr. Carnal-Security. Indeed. He is a rogue. Let's take him apart. Well, let's be realistic and see what Webster has to say. viz. "Carnal: Of the body or flesh—opposed to spiritual—of the body as the seat of appetites—sensual, specifically, sexual." Well, let's be just general. And let's say, "Confidence in the flesh." And that alone is enough to give anyone trouble without going any further.

Well, Mr. Carnal-Security lived in Mansoul and he was as charming a chap as you could ever hope to meet. Bunyan says he entertained royally. And the temptation to go to his parties was more than poor Will and Understanding and Conscience could bear. They didn't do anything terribly wrong. They just got so involved with him that . . .

The prince waited for Will and Understanding and Conscience to come to his castle as they used to. Usually, they didn't come. Sometimes they came but they were restless and hurried and anxious to get away. Their visits to the prince became shorter. And shorter.

Is that the way it is with you? Your prayer time, that used to be so wonderful, has become a duty to breeze through automatically and begone. You are vaguely disappointed in it and you don't know why. But the most subtle and hard-to-put-your-finger-on problem can be that slowly and insidiously your old reliance on yourself ("confidence in the flesh") has sneaked back.

And the most REASONABLE argument for it is, "there is no harm in feeling confident." No. Unless you are so confident in yourself that you no longer need your Lord.

Think about it. Are you really relying on yourself . . . your nimble wit . . . your personality . . . your ability to lead . . . your popularity with the teen-agers at school and at church?

If your prayer time has become a duty the reason could be as simple as that. "Without ME. . . . ye can do nothing. . . ."

For I know that in me (that is, in my flesh,) dwelleth no good thing . . . (Rom. 7:18)

Don't
wait
too
long

So your prayer time HAS become a duty. And, in spite of yourself, you can't seem to get around to doing anything about it. Well don't let it wait too long. Let's see what happened, in Bunyan's tale, to Will and Conscience and Understanding.

They were vaguely unhappy about the prince. They did have their twinges. And each time they had a twinge, they went back to the castle and knocked on the door. But nobody answered. And because they were in a hurry, for they had a dinner-date with that absolutely fascinating Mr. Carnal-Security, they fidgeted awhile and then went away. Feeling uncomfortable, of course, but what ELSE could they do? The prince didn't answer. And because he did not answer at once, they dashed off. And the twinge got smaller and smaller until it was not troublesome at all. After all, Mr. Carnal-Security was SUCH a charming chap.

They weren't really doing anything WRONG. In fact, everything was going very well. They were confident, happy, successful. And they had all the blessings they'd enjoyed before—ever since the prince had come to stay in their midst to rule over them.

And then—

One night Mr. Carnal-Security gave a huge banquet—his mansion was ablaze with light—the tables were groaning with food—and everyone there was happy. Will and Understanding and Conscience were there and everything was going very well until—

Well, according to Bunyan, Mr. Carnal-Security had invited Mr. Godly Fear, hoping to butter him up and win him over. Mr. Godly-Fear attended, all right, but for reasons of his own. He refused the cordial mixed for him by Mr. Forget-Good— (Ah, Bunyan—aren't his allegorical characters delicious?) and promptly got into an argument with Mr. Carnal-Security.

"Oh come ON, now," said Mr. Carnal-Security. "Take a sip of the cordial—and you'll—eh—get into the spirit of the thing." "How," said Mr. Godly-Fear, refusing the cordial, "can the people of Mansoul be so merry when they are in such danger?"

And that is just the point.

In the midst of all their merriment, they were indeed in danger. Grave danger. And the awful part was, they did not know it. If your prayer time HAS become a duty, you are indeed, whether or not you know it, in danger.

In danger of depending upon your looks, your sharp personality, your popularity, your abilities. . . .

How subtle Satan is. And how much you need your Lord to SEE how subtle Satan is. Don't wait too long. Ask yourself, now, quite honestly (and it is so hard to be honest with ourselves) if you are an innocent dupe of old Mr. Carnal-Security. Confidence in yourself, instead of your Lord. . . .

It's a hard question. And it demands an honest answer.

. . . Be not wise in your own conceits. (Rom. 12:16)

"I'm
still going strong"

Are you? Well Indeed. Those are famous last words.

Let's see what happened at the banquet of Mr. Carnal-Security.

"Sip the cordial of Mr. Forget-Good," suggested that old reprobate, "it'll take a weight off your mind."

"I DO have something on my mind," said Mr. Godly-Fear, scraping his chair back, "for the people of Mansoul." And, praise be, before Mr.

Carnal-Security could stop him, he cried, "You—elders, chiefs of Mansoul—it is strange to see you so merry when Mansoul is in such danger!"

"You look ill," Mr. Carnal-Security offered, "If you want to retire . . . "

"No, I don't want to retire. Mr. Carnal-Security, how could you do what you've done to these people? You have stripped Mansoul of her strength and broken down her gates, and left her wide open to the enemy."

"I've done nothing of the sort. Mr. Godly-Fear, what IS the matter with you? Why are you so timid? I'm on your side, only you're for doubting and I'm for being confident."

"Confident of WHAT?" Ah, THAT, was a question.

"Mansoul is undefeatable!" cried Mr. Carnal-Security.

"Mansoul WAS undefeatable . . . but . . . on ONE condition . . . "

Well, by that time, the great hall was silent. Everyone was listening. Will, Understanding and Conscience were listening. What was the "one condition?" And then they heard it.

Mr. Godly-Fear said solemnly, " . . . complete dependence on the prince."

It was a bombshell. No one could speak. And there was a great silence.

There should be a great silence in your heart right now. If you are depending on yourself, your personality, your wit, your charm, your looks, even your own spirituality. . . . there should be a great silence.

"But why," you cry, "did He GIVE me all these

gifts if He doesn't want me to use them?"

Now that's a reasonable question. Why indeed.

Are you endowed with good looks? A great personality? Wit? Charm? A good figure? A good mind? All are yours, and more . . . but never forget that, whatever you have, God gave it to you. And He gave it to you, wanting, LONGING, for you to have the good sense to use it for Him.

He wants to take these gifts . . . and they ARE gifts . . . and use them to His glory.

"Every good and every perfect gift is from above."

Without their prince, they could do nothing. Without your Lord, no matter what your gifts . . . you can do nothing (of eternal value).

It is worth thinking about . . .

Every good gift and every perfect gift is from above . . .
(James 1:17)

"I didn't know it was that serious"

So you're depending on yourself? And your prayer time has become routine? But you're still "going strong?" And it has never occurred to you that it is dangerous? Well, let's get along with Bunyan's tale . . .

Mr. Godly-Fear turned to the others in the great banquet-hall. "Do you question that your strength is gone?" he cried. And then as he looked at them, up one table, down the next—"I see the question in your faces. Well, I'll answer your question with a question."

And the question he asked is one that should make you think . . . and think . . . and think again, honestly, without excuses, without pretenses, without argument. Just to think, quietly, on your knees alone with God, with all defenses down . . .

The great hall was quiet, waiting for Mr. Godly-Fear to go on. Just waiting. "Where IS the prince?" he cried.

Are you asking that? Well, where IS God? Where is Jesus Christ? My prayer times have become sterile and routine and futile and useless . . . and I'm all mixed-up and wondering whether this whole thing is even REAL . . .

"Well," Mr. Godly-Fear went on, "When did you see him last? When did you sit at his table for a feast? When have you looked for him . . . really earnestly looked for him? When have you talked with him—REALLY talked with him? When have you seen his face?"

And there was no answer.

"You do not answer . . . you cannot answer. Well, I'll answer for you." And the great banquet hall was quiet. All the people were quiet. Will was quiet. And Understanding. And Conscience. Waiting. And Mr. Godly-Fear shouted . . . "He's GONE!"

And they waited, shocked.

"He's gone," he said in a whisper. "You were too busy for him and he's gone . . . "

And they waited.

"And you do not even know . . . when . . . he left."

And they waited.

"Oh, Will. . . . Understanding. . . . Conscience . . . you have been feasting with the one who has driven your lord away. . . . "

And they were shocked into a terrible silence. Not one of them could answer.

You did not know it was that serious? Well it is. You can go on about your way, with your charming personality, your popularity, your wit, and never even know that your Prince is gone. And the horrible part is, you do not even know when He left.

And how does that leave you? Pretty empty. " . . . broken cisterns, that can hold no water." (Jer. 2:13)

He will never really leave you. But you can lose the sense of His presence, His nearness, by your own indifference.

It is something to think about.

For my people have committed two evils; they have forsaken me the fountain of living waters, and hewed them out cisterns, broken cisterns, that can hold no water. (Jer. 2:13)

"What's
the
problem?"

Well, what WAS the problem?

Mr. Conscience, bless his honest heart, got to his feet at last. "I . . . ," and he was trembling so that he could scarcely stand. "I—Mr. Godly-Fear, I cannot answer your question. I have not seen my prince for a long time. I've been . . . so busy. I—well, I can't remember—when I saw him last. Everything you say is true. Everything."

Well that was a large statement. For Mr. Godly-Fear had told them that their defenses were down —their gates were down—that while they were feasting, they were already wide open to the enemy.

Conscience sank back into his seat. Mr. Godly-Fear looked down the banquet tables and searched the pale faces of the other elders and officers. Not one of them could meet his eyes.

Mansoul is you. And all the ones at the banquet

are parts of you. Will and Understanding and Conscience, you know well. They are the most important parts of you. The other ones at the banquet you may not know as well. But they are parts of you too. The million little character-traits that make up your personality—that make you YOU.

When did YOU see Him last? When did you talk with Him—really talk with Him? Or have you been—busy?

So busy with yourself—your popularity—your talents—that you haven't had time to "go to the castle"—to be with Him alone.

These very talents are gifts from Him. The very things that are keeping you away from Him are the things He has given you. And He gave them to you wanting—yes longing for you to use them for Him. He has such hopes for you. Such plans for you.

If your prayer time has become a duty, your problem is yourself. Know now, that everything you have and everything you are belongs to Him.

Did you ever read the Song of Solomon? You should. It's a beautiful story of a lover and his beloved. And the problem in the Song of Solomon is that the beloved became so absorbed in the gifts her lover gave her—that she did not have time for Him—the GIVER of the gifts. The very gifts kept her away from Him.

Don't let the gifts God gave you keep you away from Him, the giver.

. . . Thy face, LORD, will I seek. (Ps. 27:8)

"Now I'm awake . . .
but . . ."

So you're awake to your problem. On to that rascal, Mr. Carnal-Security who got you so involved. And you've decided to denounce the culprit and get back to the real business at hand. But it isn't as easy as you'd expected. It just isn't that pat. And you're disappointed. Why is life so complicated?

Well, let's see what happened to Mansoul, in Bunyan's tale. After Mr. Godly-Fear's outburst, they rose to a man and denounced Mr. Carnal-Security and shouted "Burn his house . . . burn HIM!" Which they promptly did. And that should have been the end of it. But it wasn't.

They went to church . . . they sent messages to the prince . . . but somehow they couldn't get through to him. "What shall we do?" they cried to Mr. Godly-Fear. And the answer he gave them was hard. "Keep on trying," he said. "It is the way of the wise prince to make you wait and exercise patience. You are the ones who have wronged him; you should be willing to wait for him to answer." But it was hard to wait. They had repented with enthusiasm, with all their hearts . . . but after that first burst was over the truth of the matter was that they simply did not have the "ole stick-to-it-iv-ness" to hang on.

And so they became sick and faint and weak. Their garments became dirty and torn—their fighting men run down. And they were an easy prey for invasion.

"WHAT invasion," you are thinking. You have repented of your big sins . . . or your big sin, as the case may be. What can "invade" you now? This waiting is discouraging.

Well, that's exactly what they thought. And while they were moping, some unconquered gremlins began to come out of hiding. Lord Anger—Lord Hate—Lord Deceit—and that old villain, Lord Covetousness. They didn't come out all at once of course. They were too clever for that. They came out little by little. Oh so timidly at first. They just barely stuck their noses out. Then they ventured out on the streets of Mansoul. And then—as no one seemed inclined to do them any harm—they came out boldly and asserted themselves.

It is wonderful to be awake to your problem, whatever it is, and get right with God. And usually it IS as simple as that. But once in awhile, for reasons we cannot understand, He DOES make us wait. Wait in darkness while our prayers seem to bounce off the ceiling.

It is no time to mope. That is when gremlins sneak out. It is no time to depend on your feelings. He is with you—whether you FEEL He is with you or not! Just get up and get going, banking on His word. For He has told you "I will **never** leave thee nor forsake thee." And He meant it. And when the darkness is past, you will suddenly realize "Why He has been there all the time!"

. . . I will never leave thee, nor forsake thee. (Heb.13:5)

"I've stumbled again"

Well pick yourself up. You are not alone.

In Bunyan's tale when the people of Mansoul had such difficulty in getting back to the prince, it was because they had forgotten one very important thing. Way back in the golden days, when the prince had first come to dwell with them, he had called them to the market-square, and there as they gathered round eagerly to listen, he had outlined his plan for government, and had explained to them what his rule was going to be like.

Now he told them many things . . . but one of the most important things was this: "And now," he said, "I have something to set you apart." And he called his attendants and they brought forth out of his treasury beautiful robes, glistening white. "These are my livery—a badge of honor—by which you will be known as mine. Keep them clean; if you soil them you dishonor me. Tuck them up in your belts—don't let them drag in the dirt. And—" and this is the important part—"if you should get them dirty, come to me quickly through the Lord Chief Secretary, and tell me about it, so that I may cleanse them again."

You get back to God by confessing your sin. Sins come in all sizes—from giant-size down to the smallest size imaginable. And the little sins need confessing as well as the big ones. What happens then? Well, God tells us: "If we confess our sins . . . He is faithful and just to forgive us our sins, and to cleanse us from all unrighteousness."

"Confess" means to own up to, to admit. You're telling God something He already knows, and he knows you know it. Of course, He just wants you to **admit** it.

And in admitting it, you are, in a sense taking your livery to Him to be cleansed. "These are my livery—a badge of honor—by which you will be known as mine. . . . "

If we confess our sins . . . (I John 1:9)

"This
is
that"

Oh the people in Mansoul had a great talent all right. They had a positive genius for kidding themselves. They thought they were being honest —when they recognized that Lord Anger was walking the streets they squashed him down and drove him back into hiding.

But do you know what he did? He waited till things blew over and they had stopped worrying about him, and then he disguised himself and out he came again. So did Lord Covetousness. Bunyan says "They clothed themselves in sheeps' russet and changed their manner of speaking and even their names, and hired out as servants to some of the most important men in Mansoul. The Lord Covetousness, that old villain, called himself Prudent-Thrifty and was hired by Mr. Mind. Lord Anger changed his name to Good-

Zeal and so on and on and on. All of them. And they found no trouble getting jobs. . . "

It's the old story of "wolves in sheeps' clothing." There is no end to these gremlins and no end to their cleverness. As long as you are on to them they are quite helpless, but if they can get you to call them something ELSE—then they have it made.

And the pity of it is, they usually can. Get you to call them something else, that is.

Did you ever hear some super-spiritual Christian say—"But I'm not angry—I never get angry—I'm simply filled with righteous indignation." Or, "But I'm not gossiping. I just wanted to share this (bit of juicy gossip) with you so you can pray about it with me. She DOES need prayer, you know." Ever been guilty of it yourself?

We have a genius for thinking this is that. This is NOT that. This is THIS. And until we can be honest enough to call it by its real name, and ask God to deal with it for what it is . . . we are in great danger of becoming that most pathetic— of all specimens—a phony Christian. Satan is never so clever than when he can get us to say "This is that."

Take yourself to God in all honesty—and ask the Holy Spirit to help you call a spade a spade. Ask Him to show you the thing as it really is, not as you fondly imagine it to be. "The heart is deceitful above all things . . . who can know it?" No one but God.

The heart is deceitful . . . (Jer. 17:9)

177

"I've gone too far"

The thing has gotten out of hand. It's too late to turn back. It's too late to get right with God. And you're pretty discouraged about it. What's the use of trying now? Well, you're right where Satan wants you. If he can keep you in that mood for the rest of your life, he'll be able to chalk up one more Christian he has rendered useless. That's just the way he likes it.

In Bunyan's tale, the people in Mansoul had that problem. They were in about as bad a shape as they could be. Their defenses were down— their gates were down—their captains were weak and sickly from lack of nourishment. The gremlins—and by now there were many of them—were wandering about the streets uncontrolled. Will and Understanding and Conscience had retreated to the castle. They were all right where Satan wanted them.

They had, however, one chance to survive, and that chance was faith. And Satan knew it. He had to act fast. He stormed up to the castle and demanded entrance. "Deliver me Captain Faith!" he shrieked. "Give me Captain Faith—and I'll go away—I'll never bother you again. I promise!"

Understanding popped his head out of an upper window and glory be, for the first time in his life he said the right thing. "Be quiet!" he shouted. "We'll resist you as long as there's a stone left in Mansoul and a captain left alive to throw it!"

And then Satan pulled his prize trick out of his bag-o-tricks. "Whom do you think you're fooling?" he cried. "The prince won't forgive you now —you've gone too far!"

Ah, that. Yes.

But Understanding clung to the one thing he **knew**—no matter how he **felt.** "Oh yes he will!" he shouted back. "He has said, 'him that cometh to me, I will in no wise cast out!' "

There was nothing more Satan could say. He has no answer for the Word of God.

Many a Christian has stopped right there. Never to grow again. But YOU don't have to. He will in no wise cast you out. He is faithful and just to forgive you your sin. He will never leave you nor forsake you. Give Him your faith, weak as it is, and ask His forgiveness.

. . . Him that cometh to me I will in no wise cast out.
(John 6:37)

179

"Doubts are always with me"

And you feel guilty about it. Don't. Doubting is a very part of your nature—it's the way you are made.

In Bunyan's tale, when Satan saw that Will and Understanding and Conscience were determined to stand fast in spite of the fact that Mansoul was in terrible shape, he decided to wage an all-out war. He mustered up a tremendous army to march on Mansoul—an army of—of all things—DOUBTERS. On and on they came, ten thousand, twenty thousand, thirty thousand, forty thousand strong. And they were led by none other than that old rascal—Unbelief! It looked hopeless.

But there was one bright spot in the darkness of Mansoul. They still had Captain Faith! And Faith knew one thing. He know that the prince would come to their rescue if they would just hang on. So he mustered all the people of Mansoul (the gremlins ran for cover!) and the fight began.

What a fight it was! Faith's enthusiasm was contagious, and they shouted cries of victory even in the face of what looked like sure-fire defeat. They fought until . . . the sound of distant trumpets! Through the smoke and dust, Captain Faith lifted his eyes and saw the prince coming—coming with colors flying—trumpets sounding—the feet of his men scarcely touching the ground! And then —

A giant pincer movement! The prince on one side, the army of Captain Faith on the other—and they slashed their way—fought their way—**prayed** their way toward each other until they met there on the plain—the doubters trampled to a pulp underneath! When the dust of battle settled—there was not one doubter left alive.

They "shouted cries of victory even in the face of what looked like sure-fire defeat."

And so must you. Do not feel guilty over your doubts. Even Bunyan himself, one of the greatest

Christians of all times admitted, in private life, to moods of secret unbelief. God understood that. And He understands it in you. All He asks of you is to keep Captain Faith alive and well-nourished. Keep your faith in good health with a proper diet. Nourish it with the Word of God.

. . . help thou mine unbelief. (Mark 9:24)

"They told me this was going to be easy"

Is the fight never over? I thought I had it made. And now this!

Well indeed.

Somebody might have told you it was going to be easy, but God never did. Jesus said very plainly "Whosoever will come after me, let him deny himself, and take up his cross, and follow me."

What happened in Mansoul after the dust was settled? The prince had come home. It should have been over. But it was not—quite. Bunyan said there was one gigantic project after another —and they couldn't do them in peace either. No. Satan rallied more fighters, just enough to give them trouble. Hardly a day went by that there wasn't a skirmish reported. And then Bunyan said something very interesting. He said that there was an up-and-coming young man who made quite a name for himself at this time— fellow by the name of Self-Denial. He made short work of many of Satan's fighters—and carried many a scar to show for it.

It is true that your Christian life can be one of joy and victory, if you depend upon the Holy Spirit of God—but it will never be one without its skirmishes. Would you really want it any other way? Anything worth while is worth fighting for. You deny yourself in order to excel in sports. You deny yourself in order to have a good figure. Those things are rewarding. But they are nothing compared with the rewards that are yours if you deny yourself for God.

So get up and fight, deny yourself your pet habits and little sins, and He will give you more in return than you could ever possibly give up!

. . . Whosoever will come after me . . . (Mark 8:34)

Diligence
of the
M.B.I.

Once the people of Mansoul got established in this new life of victory, they went all-out to keep it that way. They even had a secret service. The Mansoul Bureau of Investigation. A typical case went something like this:

Some shadowy figures met just outside ear-gate and sneaked to the home of Mr. Evil-Questioning, who was in charge of Satan's underground in Mansoul. He opened his squeaky door and let them in. They were just settling down for a good talk when there was pounding on the door. "Open up in the name of the king!"

Mr. Evil-Questioning hustled his spies into a

closet and then opened the door with a face as innocent as a lamb. "Yessssss, gentlemen?"

"You are all under arrest. You are Mr. Evil-Questioning?"

"There must be some mistake, gentlemen. My name is not Evil-Questioning. My name is Honest-Inquiry." (Isn't Satan subtle?)

"Tell that to the judge. Your name is Evil-Questioning, you're smuggling doubters — and you're wanted in the name of the king."

"And who might you be, my good man?"

"Diligence, of the M.B.I. Inspector Diligence to you. Take them away, sergeant."

Yes, Mansoul went all-out.

And so must you. God wants you to be "diligent." Diligent means pains-taking. To give a thing your **careful** attention. And the most important thing in life to you is to give careful attention to this new life in Christ that God has given you. "The soul of the sluggard" just wants and has nothing. " . . . but the soul of the **diligent**" is made prosperous . . . !

The soul of the sluggard desireth, and hath nothing: but the soul of the diligent . . . (Prov. 13:4)

The Case of the Elusive Ghost

This fascinating underground work you do as a Christian goes on and on. There is no end to it. In the files of the M. B. I. were some pretty strange cases. The case of Mr. Clip-Promise—he was wanted for embezzlement. The case of Mr. Live-by-Feeling, the case of No Hope. And on and on.

There was one very peculiar case—called the case of the Elusive Ghost. Fellow by the name of

Mr. Carnal-Sense. Now this fellow had been captured time and time again. But he always mysteriously escaped. First thing you knew he'd been seen around town again. He had a habit of cropping up most unexpectedly. He was often captured, yes, but never for keeps. His case was never closed.

And so it is with you in your Christian life. Mr. Carnal-Sense. You may have clobbered Mr. Carnal-Security (Confidence in the flesh) but Mr. Carnal-Sense? You will never finish him off. He's there to stay. For he is awareness of the flesh, and that, as long as you're here on earth, you will have to contend with. You can squash it down, but it will crop up again in a million sneaky disguises, to haunt you as long as you live. Awareness of yourself, your pride, your talents, your looks, your feelings.

What to do? Just keep on giving it to God. Reckon it **dead.** In other words, **count** it dead. It is not as discouraging as it sounds. Once you get the habit, you can spot it a mile away through most of its disguises, and squash it right down again. You can be "Dead indeed unto sin . . . but alive unto God."

Romans 6:11

"What is God up to?"

What exactly is God trying to do in your life? Why does He allow sin to plague you like gnats flying about your face? What does He expect of you? What are you to believe about Him? What is He up to?

The people of Mansoul wondered about these things too. They wondered, for instance, why some of the gremlins were allowed to crop up to trouble them. And here Bunyan wrote some of the most beautiful words perhaps ever written, aside from the Bible itself. The prince told them —"It is to keep thee watchful—to try thy love. I have loved thee, Mansoul: I bought thee with my blood, and stood by thee when thou wert unfaithful. Yes—I did, though thou didst not understand.

"It was I who made your way dark and bitter after thou didst sin . . . it was I who put Mr. Godly-Fear to work—it was I who stirred up your will and your understanding and your conscience —it was I who made you seek me, and in finding me, you found your own happiness.

"Nothing can hurt thee but sin . . .

   "Nothing can grieve me but sin . . .

      "Nothing can make thee fall before thy
         foes but sin . . .

"Beware of sin, my Mansoul.

"I will pray for thee . . . I will fight for thee.

"I have taught thee to watch, to fight, to pray; now I command thee to believe that my love is constant toward thee. Oh my Mansoul, how I have set my heart, my love upon thee.

"Show me thy love—and hold fast—until I take thee to my Father's kingdom where there is no sorrow—no grief—no pain—

"Where thou shalt never be afraid again. . . "

If ye love me, keep my commandments. (John 14:15)